MW00577630

THE PERFECT SOUTHERN FRATERNITY PARTY

THE PERFECT

SOUTHERN

FRATERNITY

PARTY

FROM **HOUSE BANDS** TO **NATIONAL ACTS,**
THE **COMPLETE GUIDE** TO **PLANNING,**
BOOKING AND **PRODUCTION**

TREY MYERS

LIONCREST
PUBLISHING

COPYRIGHT © 2016 TREY MYERS

All rights reserved.

THE PERFECT SOUTHERN FRATERNITY PARTY

*From House Bands to National Acts, the Complete Guide
to Planning, Booking, and Production*

ISBN   978-1-61961-542-7 *Paperback*

978-1-61961-543-4 *Ebook*

This book is dedicated to Mike Dillard and Travis Wolfe: the former for inspiring me to write a book, the latter for being a constant source of guidance, inspiration, and friendship.

CONTENTS

—

INTRODUCTION

CONGRATULATIONS, YOU'RE THE SOCIAL CHAIR. NOW WHAT?

Your job as a social chair is to throw great parties. You will stand and fall on your ability to achieve this goal. You need to manage, and therefore exceed, expectations, so that everyone who comes to a party you have organized leaves thrilled (with the exception of anyone who gets so blackout drunk they can't remember what they saw; that's on them).

You have been elected to the position of social chair because your peers believe that you have the talent and application to make a success of the role. Now you need to convince between fifty and 150 people in your chapter that you'll bring them the best bang for their buck.

What does that mean?

It means great entertainment. It means having parties that bring status to your fraternity. It means getting girls there.

You want your parties to be memorable, for everyone to have a good time, and for those who aren't fortunate enough to attend to envy those who are.

A great show provokes FOMO (fear of missing out) and brings bragging rights to your fraternity. It'll blow up on social media and be something you're talking about for years to come. To produce a show of that quality, you must be a master of managing expectations.

The vast majority of people know nothing about putting together an outstanding party. If they did, they'd be doing your job. All they want is to show up to something awesome.

Often, their expectations of what's possible are totally unrealistic. You're the one who needs to inject a sense of realism into proceedings, manage their options, and bring them incredible shows, all working within your available budget. Doing that successfully requires a lot of finesse and a lot of discipline.

This can be a thankless task. Executing a great show means

that you need to be on the ball on the day of the event. You can't just kick back with your buddies and trust that it will all run smoothly. It won't. There will be last-minute hitches and complications. There always are.

If you've taken on the role of social chair to impress girls and build the profile of yourself and your chapter, you'll find that the true benefits often come further down the line, when you have time to look back on what you've accomplished. At the time, you're going to be so swamped by the workload that you won't have time to enjoy the spoils of victory.

Understand that unless you choose to sub out, which means taking an active role in the planning process but delegating responsibility for the day of show operations, this is what you've signed up for. If you do choose to sub out, there are a number of ways to do that, which we'll discuss later in this book.

Whatever approach you take, you'll need to master the art of delegation at some stage. When there are three different tasks that need doing at the same time, you must be realistic about what you can achieve and be prepared to hand off some of the responsibility.

As a social chair, you have three choices:

1. Execute your event yourself and gain the satisfaction that comes from a job well done, but miss out on enjoying it.

2. Execute your event yourself, enjoy it with your buddies, and watch as something crucial goes wrong.

3. Hire someone to work your event for you.

Before you start, be honest with yourself about what you're hoping to achieve. If you love to plan and execute events, and you get a buzz from watching everything happen smoothly and knowing it was your doing, you're exactly the right person to run operations on the day of show.

If you prefer to relax with your girlfriend and watch the band that you've worked so hard to book perform, recognize that you need to hire someone to take the strain.

WHAT HAPPENS IF I SCREW UP?

Let's be honest. If you make a mess of this role, you'll be ostracized socially and lose the respect of your peers. You'll also attract the mockery of people younger than you, who will see that what you're capable of is not impressive and will have no reason to show you respect.

Failing to plan and execute great shows also reflects poorly on your entire chapter, which you were elected to represent. You joined a fraternity because you want to be part of something greater than yourself, and it's vital that you honor the responsibilities you're charged with. Otherwise, you're not only letting yourself down. You're letting your brothers down, too.

Your fraternity brothers elected you to this post because they believe you can handle it, and they know that they can't. If you don't fulfill your responsibilities, you'll tarnish your own reputation and the reputation of your entire fraternity. That's not a position you want to put yourself in.

Whatever people are hoping to achieve through the social calendar—whether that be to have an amazing time, to meet girls, or to host events that will be talked about for years to come—is in your hands. Fail to get it done, and you'll be robbing yourself and your brothers of those experiences. No pressure.

WHY SHOULD YOU LISTEN TO ME?

Excelling as a social chair is tough. If you want to succeed (and if you're reading this book, you surely do), then you'll need the help of someone who has done this hundreds of times before: someone who knows how to take an ordinary event and turn it into an epic experience.

That someone is me.

I worked for years as a booking agent, representing regional acts with an emphasis on artist development. Prior to that I worked in small venues where I participated in the talent buying process. At the time, I'd barely set foot in a fraternity house.

It was only when I moved to Athens, Georgia, that I realized just how big fraternities were. I wanted to get my bands performing at fraternity parties both because of the obvious financial potential and because I quickly realized that bands who were open to performing at fraternities had a tremendous opportunity to grow their fan bases.

Initially, I approached Greek life with the intention of building the profile of the acts I represented. It soon became clear to me, however, that the majority of events were very poorly organized, that agents and service providers were taking advantage of the naiveté of their clients, and that there was a much better way of conducting business.

The solution I arrived at wasn't complicated. It was centered on accountability and on taking away the conflicts of interest that dominated the arena.

When I started, I didn't know a great deal about running a production company. I soon understood, however, that most great technicians aren't good business people. The guys who are highly skilled at making things look and sound good are, generally speaking, way out of their depth when communication skills are required.

Similarly, the majority of agents and brokers in the field are not blessed with the highest ethical standards. They want to make as much money as they can, and they're willing to cut costs at every juncture to pad their pockets.

I saw a need for an organization that benefited from all aspects of putting on a successful event. At that time, the music industry was in flux due to the advent of download-able music. The fallout from the disruptive effect Napster had on the music industry continued to linger, and many, many acts who would not have previously seen performing at a fraternity house as a viable option were beginning to reconsider.

Private events are more lucrative for bands than ticketed events, and they saw the opportunity both to generate additional income and to attract new fans.

It has been a slow progression, but the center of gravity has gradually shifted. Twenty years ago, Greek events were populated primarily by jam bands and party bands. Nowadays, headlining rock 'n' roll bands and high-quality rap acts are open to performing for fraternities. Especially over the past few years, there has been a tremendous shift toward seeing fraternity gigs as a legitimate part of a band's itinerary.

Today, there are no barriers to what's possible. Social chairs with enough time, money, and ambition can contemplate booking the biggest acts in the country.

Turnipblood Entertainment was formed in 2011 and has carved out a niche by consistently presiding over high-quality events. The company doesn't have a vested interest in the size of the show or the profile of the band. We're responsible for the success of the entire event, and we're paid on that basis.

We thrive on exceeding expectations and making the seemingly impossible a reality. My most personally satisfying experiences have involved convincing artists who would usually never even consider playing in a fraternity house to do so, blowing the minds of the attendees.

Here's an example. Big Gigantic is an EDM (electronic dance music) duo that built their audience through the Greek scene, playing fraternities and using the proceeds to tour and to write new music. They've become very, very successful, to the extent that they can now sell out consecutive nights at Red Rocks Amphitheatre in Colorado, an outdoor venue with a ticket cap of ten thousand people.

Naturally, booking them has been well out of the reach of the average fraternity party for the past couple of years. We convinced them to perform in a three-hundred-capacity living room inside a fraternity house.

They were between record cycles, and the gig was billed as a chance for them to return to their roots and get back to the kind of venues that gave them their initial boost. From their perspective, it was easy money and a great PR stunt. For us, it was a massive, massive coup and a night I'll never forget. We had so much production that the house was literally moving. I've worked bigger shows, with bigger name acts, but I've never put a larger act into a smaller space.

As much as I love to pull off the impossible, I'm also motivated by turning people on to up-and-coming bands and acts that I know will be huge in a year or two. The experience I've gleaned working in the industry pays off hugely here. Turnipblood has a very strong network, and we specialize in pairing fraternities that don't have a huge budget with amazing acts they'll be bragging about hosting within a couple of years.

We've convinced people to take on acts that have subsequently become huge international names, giving them the opportunity to say: "You know those guys who were playing at the Georgia Theater last night? We had them perform on our porch." That's an exceptionally rewarding part of doing this work.

WHAT WILL YOU GET OUT OF THIS BOOK?

The idea for this book was born when I moved to Athens, Georgia, and got a good look under the hood at the way fraternity parties were being planned and executed.

Most fraternities engaged multiple vendors, all of whom had an agenda. That's not to say that the vendors were behaving dishonestly, but merely that the guy who rents lights has a vested interest in renting out as many lights as possible, and the guy who books bands inevitably wants to book the most expensive bands possible. There was an inherent conflict of interest.

I realized that a turnkey approach to booking parties, with the event as the central focus, had the potential to bring enormous value to the customer. We gave social chairs a one-stop shop for every aspect of producing an event, with no stake in whether they booked a large entertainer or a small entertainer, or whether they held their party on a large outdoor stage or in the band room of their fraternity house.

Contained within these pages is all the information you need to successfully execute a private event. This book can't run your show for you, but it can give you all the information you need.

You'll find a step-by-step approach that covers exactly what you need to do to plan, book, and execute an outstanding southern fraternity party. This is the play-by-play. With this book in your hands, you'll be prepared to handle any situation you encounter in the process of putting together a private event.

Use this book however you see fit. Read it from cover to cover, or dip in to find the answers to specific questions. Start at the end and read backward if you like. If you find yourself reading through part two and getting bogged down in the process, skip to part three and learn how to sub out. If you want to nail the execution yourself, read part two and plan like a pro. If you prefer to delegate, read part one and hand off part two to one of your fraternity brothers.

There's really no wrong way to read this book. You can even keep it somewhere visible in your room, so that people think you know what you're doing, and never open it.

Ready? Let's plan some parties.

PART ONE

—

PLANNING

"The best way to predict the future is to create it."
ABRAHAM LINCOLN

"Proper planning prevents piss poor performance."
MILITARY ADAGE

HOW NOT TO THROW A PARTY

—

Being a social chair is a dream come true: social status, great times, the adulation of your fraternity brothers, and all the girls you can meet. Until it all goes wrong, of course.

Read through this list of seven party disasters, all of which I've seen firsthand, and ask yourself what you would do to prevent them from happening or how you would handle them when they arose. If you don't know, you need this book. You'll find answers and guidance below.

1. What happens if the rapper shows up and is not the person you paid for?

2. What happens when the rapper you paid for gets pulled over for weed two hours outside town and doesn't show?

3. What happens when the DJ you hired doesn't have the appropriate equipment to perform?

4. What happens when a band shows up and you don't have the backline they need?

5. What happens when the artist you just paid $10,000 to plays for twenty minutes and quits?

6. What happens when an unhappy neighbor calls the police?

7. What happens when you blow your budget on entertainment, then realize you don't have the funds to provide tech or hospitality rider requirements?

What would you do? Take a moment to think about your responses, then I'll share some tips on how to stay cool and handle these kinds of situations when they go down.

1. What happens if the rapper shows up and is not the person you paid for?

This has happened to me, with a hip-hop act hired to perform at a university in the Southeast. About three hours before they were due to show up, the front man's social media was blowing up—in LA. Unless he was shaping to get on a rocket ship, there was no way he was getting to the show in time.

We were speaking to the guy's entourage, and they were coming in. They didn't know that we knew the headliner wasn't with them. Fortunately, we had an advantage because we knew in advance that the headliner wasn't going to show.

We could have called them on it before they even arrived, but we'd already paid them a deposit. If we alerted them to the potential for conflict, there would have been a high probability of their simply turning tail and not showing up at all.

Instead, we let them get to the venue, unload their gear, and get ready to perform. When they were about go on stage, we said to them: "Listen, we know the headliner's not here. You know that's not right. We're going to have to address this, and we're not going to pay you the full fee. Go out there and perform, and we'll settle up after the show."

At that point, they were faced with the option of making some money versus no money. They'd already received a 50 percent deposit, and we ended up paying them 50 percent of the remaining balance. It wasn't what people wanted, and we'll never work with them again, but they did perform.

Knowing that rap is a comparatively volatile genre, we'd also hedged our bets by booking a well-known DJ as a warm-up act, which also eased the pain of not having the headliner show.

2. What happens when the rapper you paid for gets pulled over for weed two hours outside town and doesn't show?

Again, I have personal experience with this. Knowing that some kind of mess is always a possibility, we had hired a jam band to warm up the crowd. Typically, a jam band can easily stretch a set, and that's what we did.

Meanwhile, we had another guy on call. He was three hours away and, while a much lesser-known act, he was a better option than disappointing people altogether. We gave him half of the money we would have paid to the headliner and kicked a small portion of what was left over to the opening band for performing a longer set.

Once again, it was less than perfect, but it was a big improvement on canceling the show.

3. What happens when the DJ you hired doesn't have the appropriate equipment to perform?

One solution is to use prerecorded music. DJs can often take a song mix, press play, and pretend to be making music on stage when in fact they're just playing a preproduced mix. Some of the biggest DJs on the planet do this all the time.

The biggest stumbling block you'll run into if you ask a DJ to do this is artistic integrity. While we appreciate artistic integrity, we also appreciate a party moving forward as scheduled, so it behooves the artist who wants to get paid and stay in the frame for future bookings to find mutually agreeable ways of getting music to people. Faking it is one of those ways.

If it's really not possible for the DJ to play prerecorded music, perhaps because the he doesn't have a thumb drive with all of his music downloaded on it, or he refuses point blank to compromise artistic integrity, it's time to crank up the music and keep the beer flowing.

What do I mean by that? You should have invested heavily in lighting and sound, so put them to work. Create an atmosphere that's bigger than the DJ.

Ask the DJ (assuming he's male) to go around and take selfies with the girls at the party. Ask him to hang out and have a drink with your fraternity brothers. Let his celebrity be the highlight of the event, rather than his music, and laugh about the fact that you didn't have the right mixer.

Usually, one of these options will pan out. It's not what you wanted, but it's still fun, and it's a lot better than nothing.

I've personally known this to happen with a national act. Everyone assumed that the other party had what was needed, and no one did, and the DJ was completely unwilling to act the part.

Fortunately, this was at a professional venue, not a fraternity house. They turned up all of their lights, blew fake snow around, and started giving away alcohol. The DJ mingled with people and took selfies.

A handful of execs in the fraternity were bent out of shape by the experience, but the average participant had an amazing time.

On another occasion, the DJ used a prerecorded mix and rocked a party for three thousand people. No one knew the difference, because it was his music and he manipulated a mixer to make it look as though he was mixing live. It worked perfectly.

This is a strategy that's used deliberately all the time, even when there's been no mistake. It's commonplace at large festivals, where people have paid a lot of money and where substandard production isn't an option.

4. What happens when a band shows up and you don't have the backline they need?

If a band shows up without a drum kit, there's clearly no faking it. You'll need to find them one from somewhere.

Start by calling up venues and anyone you know that plays in a band. Usually, in a college town, there's a drum kit lying around somewhere. It may not be the best kit in the world, but you don't need the best. You need a drum kit you can use.

Most other backline can be run direct and won't require stage amplification, so you can certainly wing it. This is not a time to start blaming people. It's a time to be polite to the artist or band, make sure that they understand the situation, and apologize for not having what they need.

At an all-day event, where we weren't responsible for organizing the backline, the headliner showed up expecting it to be provided. It wasn't. We reached out to the band that had just finished their set. We offered them booze and pizza while the headliners used their gear to play a set. For a smaller band, having the opportunity to kick it with a larger band, when they had nowhere special to be, was a good opportunity.

That kind of approach can be adapted. In a college town,

there's probably a band performing at a dive bar some-where. Get ahold of them and invite them to hang out with the band, talk to some girls, and watch a great show while their gear is onstage for ninety minutes. They'll probably go for it.

5. What happens when the artist you just paid $10,000 to plays for twenty minutes and quits?

This is simple. If you've paid a 50 percent deposit to an act to perform for an hour, and they've walked off stage after twenty minutes, they've only fulfilled a third of their obligation. Don't give them another dime.

Tell them that their options are to leave peacefully and maybe work another show, or cause problems that require involving the police, thereby guaranteeing that you'll never work with them again.

If you've already paid them, you're in a bind, unless you're in a position to physically recover the money. Holding gear hostage can reintroduce leverage, but don't pull gangster moves unless you're ready to be treated like a gangster. You can go through the courts, but it's a long, costly process. This is why it's a smart idea to work with honorable people and to resist paying people who haven't been vetted 100 percent up front.

Understand the position of your artists. They've probably been screwed over twenty times, and that's why they want to be paid up front. Do this job for any length of time, however, and you'll get screwed over, too, which is why you want to hold back paying people in full until successful completion of the show.

The best solution is to meet in the middle. Offer a 50 percent deposit and 50 percent when they walk off stage. If people won't agree to that, it's a red flag. Numerous times, especially with hip-hop artists, I've encountered people who expect to be paid up front.

I make it very clear to artists that because I have already given them 50 percent of their fee in the form of a deposit, I expect them to repay my show of good faith by delivering an amazing show.

I guarantee that I'll be standing by the side of the stage with a sack of money, and that it will be theirs as soon as they perform the last note of their set. I give them my word that all the money will be there, and I request that they understand where I'm coming from, just as I understand where they're coming from.

If they're not willing to bend, there's a high probability that they are not trustworthy.

There is a risk that you'll start a battle of wills. They can threaten to leave just as easily as you can threaten not to pay them. The reality of the situation, however, is that they came to play.

Everyone involved should want the show to happen. If they don't, why are they there? Usually, offering to meet in the middle provides a compromise everyone can live with.

A couple of years ago, I worked with an artist who wanted cash. We had agreed to pay them with a check, and our checks are as good as any on the planet, but their manager was telling us that they wouldn't perform without cash.

I explained to them that they had two options: They could take the check, perform well, and stay in the loop for further business, or they could walk away and never work with us again. They took the check.

To an extent, their concerns were legitimate. Checks don't always clear, and it turned out that they didn't have a bank account. They called me at 2:00 a.m. that night from a check-cashing depot, where they were paying upwards of 25 percent to get their check cashed.

Always be willing to adapt. If they'd come to me with a good reason why they needed cash, I would have listened.

Instead, they were confrontational. They were also one of seven acts performing that day, so I was willing to let them walk.

On another occasion, an established act came to me calmly and explained why he needed cash. My first inclination was to refuse, but I realized that would be sheer stubbornness. I swallowed my pride, paid him in cash, and he performed an amazing set.

Don't allow yourself to get gypped, but don't be so bull-headed that you gyp other people. As a social chair, your first loyalty is to making a great show happen.

6. What happens when an unhappy neighbor calls the police?

If the police show up, the damage has been done, because they're legally bound to cite you. Your best bet is to get an extremely sober representative to speak with the police officer and ask what you can do to continue the show.

You need to demonstrate that you're 100 percent willing to cooperate. The officer may tell you that there's nothing he or she can do because the music is too loud and the hour is too late. Alternatively, the officer may say that if you can turn it down, or wrap it up within the next twenty minutes, you can keep it going.

The very last thing you want to do is start telling an officer of the law what you will and won't do. The police have the authority to lock you up, lock the sound guy up, and haul the band off to jail. Realize that you are not in control, that you created this situation, and that you need to ask for help.

Turning the music down substantially actually has a significant positive effect. It forces people closer to the stage, which can lead to a much more engaged crowd. Unlike ticketed events, where people have paid money to be in attendance, the natural tendency at social events is to mingle with friends and wander around. A good soundman should already be aware of this and adjust volume levels accordingly.

You can even try talking to the band and asking them whether they're willing to perform an acoustic set, move inside, or shift venues. Many larger acts won't even consider that, but money is a great motivator. Paying a party band or a jam band an extra $1,000 to spend forty-five minutes moving their gear indoors, or allowing sober people to move their gear indoors, could be a solution.

Another option is to invite the police officer to walk the perimeter of the event with you and measure sound levels. The officer should have a device for measuring sound levels on his or her person and can compare the number of decibels with the maximum permitted levels.

If you can be humble, while simultaneously demonstrating that you're in the right, there's a chance you can convince an officer of the law to call the station and report that you're not breaking the law, that you're willing to comply with his guidelines, and that you've turned the music down. That can be the difference between continuing your party and having to shut it down.

The best fallback plan available to you is to actually hire a cop to be present at your event. This is not because he's going to act as a security guard. He's not. He's going to sit there and talk to girls all night.

The reason you want him there is that he has a radio. A radio is magic in this situation, because if someone calls the police station, the station can then call him before a squad car is deployed, and he can tell you to turn the music down.

If the police need to show up at your event, they are bound by law to issue you with a citation, so your friend with a radio acts as an early warning system. By telling you if someone calls the cops, and radioing back to his colleagues on the force to tell them the disturbance has been quelled, he can prevent them from ever arriving and save you a lot of trouble.

In short: Pay a guy $25 an hour to sit there, talk to girls, and run point on any disturbances in the neighborhood. It'll be money well spent.

In most cases, the police don't want to mess up your party for kicks, but they have a responsibility to protect and serve. That can actually work to your advantage. A while ago, we had a huge, huge rap act scheduled to play. Before they had even hit town, they had garnered a lot of negative publicity. When they arrived, they were two hours late.

The crowd was frenzied, intoxicated, and already annoyed that the show was so delayed. As soon as the act got on stage, neighbors started calling the police, and inevitably they came and wanted to shut us down.

We apologized profusely, explained that we had tried to bring the act in on time, but that they had ignored our requests. We showed them two thousand drunk, crazed people, and we allowed them to come to the realization that if we cut the show, there was going to be a riot.

They understood that, recognized that if they took the act off stage, then people would get hurt, and let the performance finish.

Another move we made was to alter the bill when we became aware that the venue was in a location where noise levels posed a potential problem. That saved us a lot of money. We knew that putting the headliner on stage was a risky endeavor, so we didn't double the risk by scheduling a warm-up act. If we'd done that, the show might have been shut down before the headliner even got up to perform.

We had a dubstep DJ slated to perform. Bass is omnidirectional, meaning it can't be pointed to avoid upsetting people. Low-end bass frequencies carry a long way. We decided to put the DJ inside because we knew that if he performed outside, there was a better than average chance that the $30,000 hip-hop act would never make it onstage.

We would happily have canceled his performance and even paid him not to play if it had been necessary to serve the greater good.

Whenever you're talking to the police, be hyperaware of who is in charge. I've been in a situation where there was a gate that needed to be closed to prevent people going backstage and damaging gear, and a police officer, for some reason, was determined that it should remain open. When he saw me close it, he threatened to arrest me.

My name, my liability, my company, my show, and my gear were on the line. He had no idea what he was talking about. On the other hand, I was no good to anybody locked up. I walked away and allowed one of my subordinates to handle it.

If you find yourself in a conversation with a police officer, listen, be honest, and ensure that you're sober. If you're not, get someone else to do the talking. Keep your drunk friends away from the area.

7. What happens when you blow your budget on entertainment, then realize you don't have the funds to provide tech or hospitality rider requirements?

If you've got a budget shortfall, hopefully you figure this out prior to the day of the show. You need to supply what an artist requires to perform, whatever that takes.

There are a number of great platforms nowadays that you can use to raise money quickly. Tilt is one. The old-school approach, passing the hat, can also work.

Remember that, for a lot of bands, a gig at a fraternity house is not their ideal booking. They may not have grown up in the area or been part of a fraternity themselves. They want to do a good show and get paid. At the very least, they want their art to be represented in the light they intended. If you're missing part of their tech rider, you need to remedy that situation.

If you really don't have what they need, or the money to provide it, you need to be extremely humble and apologetic, and ask them what you can do to make the show work. Explain the benefits of salvaging the show. Perhaps your fraternity has chapters all over the southeast of the country, and you can sell them on the potential for future opportunities.

The most common fubar we're called in to correct is the lack of a stage. Social chairs get a tech rider that includes a stage, and they think: "Cool, we have a stage."

Not in the eyes of a regional or a national act, they don't. They have a small sectional platform that one of their fraternity brothers built two years previously. It's been sitting in the rain since it was built. You wouldn't want to put your dog on it, let alone six or seven grown men and a thousand pounds of gear.

Stages collapse every week, people get hurt, and gear gets damaged. It's a very real danger. Time and time again, people think they're covered, but they don't understand that a rickety stage that their buddy's three-piece jam band will happily play on for a Wednesday night gig is not a stage that a national act will agree to perform on.

As a backup scenario, consider relocating them to the porch

of your fraternity house. People can stand in the yard, and the porch provides an elevated platform. Alternatively, perhaps the topography of the yard is conducive to using what staging you have got as a drum riser. Put the drummer on it, and the band can play on the ground.

These kinds of deals will likely require you to be very convincing, but I've seen them come off, many times. Once again, this is where proper planning prevents piss poor performance. Bands usually understand that, when they play at a fraternity house, the lighting and sound won't necessarily be venue-grade.

Staging, however, is a matter of safety. It's very easy nowadays to send pictures and specs and ask people whether the stage you already have meets their needs. Don't wait until they show up and tell you they're not willing to go up there.

THE BOTTOM LINE

Unless you're an experienced event planner, with expertise in the specific genres of entertainers in question, the likelihood that you're going to be able to successfully execute an audible on any of these plays is very slim.

The reality of these situations is that they need to be caught on the front end, and handling them is an advanced skill. That being said, there are always things you can do to limit the damage. When you understand what might go wrong, you can put in place backup plans that limit the possibility of a disaster on your watch.

Disasters such as the ones listed above happen *all the time* in Greek life. If you don't want to become a statistic, then plan properly, and you won't suffer the consequences of piss poor performance.

In the following chapters, I'll take you step-by-step through the planning and execution of a quality event, from budgeting to booking to the day of the show. No more excuses. It's time to prepare.

THE PARTIES YOU'LL PLAN

—

All fraternities are different, but they're also largely the same. Different branches, at different schools, are connected, and they run similar calendars, with a similar objective: to impress.

You may want to impress girls. You may want to impress parents. You may want to impress alums, or future members of your fraternity. One thing's for sure, however: Regardless of your location or size, you want to impress.

No matter whether you're elected in November or May, you face a major hurdle almost as soon as you accept the role. If you're elected in November, you have the Christmas break ahead of you. Everyone whose opinion you want to seek out, and there are plenty of people, will be difficult to contact for those several weeks. You'll be separated from feedback, without access to the checkbook, and stewing on your responsibilities alone.

In May, you can expect people to leave for Europe or Mexico for the summer or to start internships. Whatever they're doing, they won't be thinking about parties in the fall, or about summer parties if those are part of your calendar. That's your job.

You need to be disciplined and confront those logistical challenges head-on, however difficult that seems. The biggest mistake a social chair can make is to procrastinate. Your responsibilities won't disappear because you go home for Christmas break or take off for a summer vacation.

These things need to happen, and you need to make sure that they're good, or you'll bring dishonor to yourself and your fraternity. This book is here to help you figure out your next steps.

PLAN LIKE A BOSS

If you have been elected in November, it's highly likely that you have a January back-to-school party to prepare for. In all probability, this won't be a huge party, but it will be happening soon.

On November 20, January 14 looks a long way away.

Between your election and your January party, however, you have finals to study for and you have to take a Christmas break. Before you know it, you'll be back at school the weekend before the party, with no band and no production. Take action *now*, not later, and you'll head off that awful sinking feeling at the pass.

You need to use the limited window available to you to get feedback from people you trust. Do *not* open up questions about which acts to book to the masses. They don't know what they're talking about. Solicit specific feedback from the people who matter.

Hopefully, your fraternity has a former social chair who you can speak to, and you have a handful of tastemakers within your inner circle who can advise you if you have any questions.

The reality, however, is that taking action at this point is far more valuable than listening to people pontificating about the best bands to book. Your first show will be happening in six weeks. A B+ show that happens beats an A+ show that never makes it out of the planning phase any day of the week.

Your next major party will probably be a February house party, perhaps featuring a large national act. The biggest problem you're facing with this scenario is that national acts typically book between three and six months out, putting you at an immediate disadvantage if you're only elected in November.

This isn't really a concern for the January party. Although party bands also need to be booked in advance, January is a slow month for weddings. As long as you're dynamic, you will probably be able to find a good Motown act or something similar at relatively short notice.

Try to book a national act for February, however, and you'll soon realize that you're dealing two to two and a half months out in a field of artists who usually book three to six months in advance. Your options will be limited before you even begin, so you'd better make some moves.

You'll also be competing with the social chairs of other fraternities, who are in exactly the same position as you. Within a three-hundred-mile radius, there may be one hundred people vying for the services of the same fifteen acts over the span of three weekends in February. Not only are many of these bands already booked, but those that are still available are suddenly in tremendous demand.

This is a situation you inherit because of the vagaries of fraternity election cycles. It's by no means your fault, but it is your responsibility to make the best of it.

The next entry in your calendar will likely be a parents' weekend, usually in March or April. You will be seeking a Motown act or some other party band to appeal to your parents and those of your fraternity brothers. In itself, this is relatively straightforward. Be aware, however, that March and April herald the beginnings of wedding season, so you will find that competition for bands is growing. This is especially true if you are holding your event on a Saturday.

It's smart to start making inquiries during the Christmas holidays. Why? Because December is a slow month for weddings. While most of the bands you'll be seeking supplement their income by playing Christmas parties, they'll nonetheless be feeling the scarcity of work compared with peak wedding season.

When people are experiencing a lag in business, they become more receptive to offers. If you approach a wedding band in the middle of December to discuss an event in March, they may be willing to work with you on pricing.

They're smart. They know that they'll be much busier in March. They may, however, be feeling the pinch when you call them, and taking your deposit check and filling up their calendar could be a very appealing proposition for them.

You're probably noticing a theme of taking action early, and for good reason. While you never want to act impulsively, you will be operating at a disadvantage for at least the first two or three months of your role. Quick, decisive action is required to make sure that you can meet your obligations. Starting dialogues and making moves early will serve you better than holding out for perfection.

The big spring party is the event of the year. It's your opportunity to show exactly what you're made of and to create an event that people will be talking about for months. Fraternity chapters become seriously competitive around the time of the spring party, and you need to make sure that yours shines.

The spring party is your magnum opus. With the exception of some fraternities in Texas that hold parties in the summer, it's the biggest event of the year. You want it to be amazing, and it deserves your full attention, advanced preparation, careful thought, and discipline. Screw this one up, and it may not matter much whether you get the others right.

Fortunately, you have the luxury of a little more time to put this event together, but that's no reason to rest on your laurels. The bigger bands that you'll be looking to book for your spring party require a lot of lead time, so organization and swift action will still be rewarded.

There are two primary approaches to your big spring party. You can book one big name act that will excite people, or you can sell the experience of an all-day festival that progresses into the evening and features several midrange bands.

The former offers a two-hour window of intense awesomeness. The latter extends the party across the entire day. Either of these options can be amazing, and your choice should be based upon an assessment of your goals.

If you're the chair of a large fraternity, you may decide that you have enough fame and notoriety, and you're more interested in creating an amazing experience for your fraternity brothers and their guests. In that case, you don't need to spend $30,000 on a rapper who'll only perform for forty-five minutes. Creating an eight-hour day festival with six $5,000 bands may be more your style.

On the other hand, perhaps you're social chair of a small fraternity and you've been saving money for a year because you want to make a splash. Perhaps your fraternity has just been released from probation and you've got a backlog of cash and a desire to change the game.

Pick the option that works for you, and remember that

booking bigger acts requires more lead time. If you want a big national act for a spring party in early April, you need to start the process in November or December and be putting in offers by the middle of January at the latest.

None of this is to say that it's impossible to book an act a month before your show. You can do it, but you'll be at a competitive disadvantage, and you'll probably pay higher prices. A band with four offers on the table will take the highest, and if that means you have to pay them top dollar or be without entertainment, you'll pay top dollar.

There's one exception to this rule, but it's not good policy. Sometimes when you wait until the last minute to approach an artist, you can get a better price on days they don't have another booking. If they have the option of sitting at home on Facebook or going out and earning $10,000, they may take the latter even if their usual price is $15,000.

Unfortunately for you, you can't rely on this approach, and if it fails, you'll be left without a band and looking like an idiot. It's a Hail Mary play, and you should use it only in very specific circumstances.

Maybe your fraternity has just been released from probation or disciplinary suspension, and you suddenly realize that you have a window for throwing a party. Maybe the dues come in at the last minute, and you have a shot at upgrading the entertainment.

In those circumstances, there's nothing to lose if the act you approach turns you down. You won't be left canceling or ruining an event, but if the play comes off, you'll feel like a hero. It's a win, or at least not a loss. In all other circumstances, the Hail Mary can't be your strategy.

On the flipside, don't try to book *too* far in advance. Big national acts don't know how successful they'll be a year ahead of time. Their next release could top the charts. For that reason, they won't want to confirm a date at their current value. Even if they do confirm, there's a high probability that they'll cancel when they get a better offer.

Throughout the year, you'll also organize numerous smaller parties such as formals and tailgates. Often, there are officers in place specifically to handle the logistics of formals and other niche events, but sometimes booking the entertainment falls to the social chair. In either scenario, you need to be capable of providing guidance where necessary.

You'll probably find yourself in the position of spearheading smaller, impromptu house parties. These usually come about because there's a surplus in the budget and a sudden enthusiasm for a party. The timescale is so truncated that you won't be able to plan far ahead, but you can still use the principles in this book to make sure that they run smoothly.

You'll also take on the September back-to-school party, which is another big deal that you need to be planning several months out, especially if you're aiming to book a national act.

If your elections take place in May, you've got three or four months to plan it, but they're the summer months. People will be out of town, traveling or doing internships. What happens when you can't contact your treasurer? How will you get the money together for a deposit? Do you even have a method of calculating your budget? Just as important, what will you do when your tastemakers aren't available to offer feedback?

You've got plenty of time before September, but none of the information you need to make an informed decision, so part of your job is to find ways of getting that information and making those decisions.

September will creep up on you. If you're elected in May, start planning straight after your election. Sit down with your trusted tastemakers, or a previous social chair, and seek their counsel. Take your role seriously.

If you were elected in November, you face the same problems of limited access to information and support, but at least you have six months of experience under your belt by the time you're coming to plan the September party. You also have the opportunity to get moving in April and take the heat out of the process.

Get some feedback, discuss what would be cool, and talk with your treasurer about the available budget—before everyone clears out for the summer and all you can hear is the sound of crickets.

Halloween parties vary a lot. Some fraternities use them as an opportunity to go all out and hire a national act. Others keep them smaller and book a more traditional band or a party band to play covers.

Whatever approach you take, know that there will probably be a lot of other people producing similar parties. The best fruit gets picked first, so don't wait around, or you'll be left with the acts no one else wants.

Your semiformals will probably call for a party band in a similar vein to the act you booked for parents' weekend. Again, you'll find that a lot of other fraternities are holding their semiformals around the same time, so it pays to get busy early.

If you've got your eye on a great band, realize that someone else has probably noticed them, too, and there are a limited number of dates available for your semiformals.

Check in with your previous social chair. Maybe he booked an act or a band that really rocked it last year, and you can get them back.

A really smart move, if you're booking an act for a March parents' weekend and you know they're awesome, is to ask them whether they'd be willing to come back in October or November for a semiformal, and knock 10 percent off their price for the bulk booking.

They might knock you back, because they make a lot of money around the time that semiformals are taking place and they don't want to book so far out, or they might bite your hand off for a 50 percent deposit six months in advance, a guaranteed gig, and the knowledge that they're working with someone who knows what they're doing. If they say yes, you kill two birds with one stone and save your fraternity some money.

If your elections take place in May, switch it around. When you're booking a band for a semiformal, make sure they're good, and offer to lock them in for parents' weekend in March if they'll give you 10 percent off. Doing this maximizes your chances of getting the acts you want, saves you a planning headache, and leaves more of your budget to spend on production or to reallocate to other parties.

A similar tactic can seriously simplify the job of putting together tailgates. Tailgates can be a pain. The football schedule isn't always out by the time you need to start planning, and even if it is, you probably don't know what time the games will be kicking off.

Usually, one tailgate takes top billing, probably due to a fierce rivalry with another school. Prioritize that one, and figure out how to divide your budget so that you have the funds for one big tailgate and several smaller ones.

Tailgates are a great opportunity to engage a middle buyer, an agent, or a turnkey company, because they can amount to as many as six bookings rolled into one. By letting them know your budget for all six, and asking them what the most effective way of spending the money is, you can make it in their interest to secure excellent deals.

Obviously, you don't want to book the same band for all six events, which is why there's not much point in approaching artists individually and asking them to cut you a deal. Asking an agent or a middle buyer to find you six acts, however, can be an extremely efficient way of using your time and resources.

The biggest tailgate, the one that stands out as the top priority, is the one to tackle first. You can either communicate that to your agent or middle buyer, or you can do the legwork yourself.

Bigger bands will probably take longer to make a decision, so work backward from the largest event and fill in the smaller ones as you go.

Organizing tailgates can be a thankless task. If the game kicks off at noon, it's hard to get people in the mood to watch a performance at 10:00 a.m. If that's the case, you'd better offer people some Bloody Marys to give them an incentive to get down there in the morning.

On the other hand, if you keep the band until after the game, there's a good chance many people will be blackout drunk from celebrating a win, or too depressed to party following a defeat.

In short, flexibility and resourcefulness are keys to running successful tailgates. Without them, you'll become very frustrated and very disheartened.

Finally, you'll undoubtedly be called upon to run numerous miscellaneous parties throughout the year. Inevitably, some will be last-minute affairs, and you'll be limited in your ability to prepare effectively.

What you can do, however, is educate yourself. As you gain knowledge and experience, remember bands that gave great performances. Keep notes about when they performed, for whom, and how much they cost. If you're working with an agent or someone who organizes events professionally, he or she will guide you. If you're doing this on your own, however, it's part of your job to keep an ongoing roster of options that you can draw from when you need to execute a last-minute event.

Doing the job of social chair puts you in a difficult situation. By the time you get good at it, you'll be handing the role on to someone else, someone who hasn't got a clue.

Some fraternities are smart and groom their social chairs a year in advance. The upcoming social chair shadows the current social chair, so that by the time he comes to take the reins, he knows what he's doing.

Others keep books and databases that you can refer to, and you always have the option of talking to the guy who did your job last year and asking for his advice. The trouble with these approaches is that the databases often aren't very good, and the previous year's social chair may be so over the job that he's glad to hand it off to someone else and wash his hands of it.

It may come down to you to break the mold and be the guy who shows the way. When a band you book gives a great show, keep a note of what you liked about them and how much they cost. If someone you know has an outstanding experience, write it down so you can remember the name of the act at a later date. It's not an easy job, but if you want to make a success of it not only for yourself but also for the honor of your fraternity in years to come, you need to do it properly.

GET ORGANIZED

The information in this chapter can be summarized in two words: *Get organized*. Evaluate the tasks you need to accomplish, and approach them methodically.

In the next two chapters you'll find all the information you need to develop your calendar and your order of operations. When you adhere to these, you won't get behind the eight ball and find yourself panicking the day before a show, or missing class because you have a big party coming up next week and you're not even halfway ready for it.

You may encounter some hurdles, and you may be handed some disadvantages, but you'll put yourself in the best possible position to handle them. As long as you approach them in the order they need to be approached, you can succeed. Get them ass-backward, and you're almost certain to fail.

If you realize that you're working inefficiently, or losing sight of your priorities, understand that won't yield a positive result and stop. Take a deep breath, consult your calendar and your order of operations, and make a course correction.

THE SOCIAL CALENDAR

—

This chapter is a summary of the likely events you'll plan and execute over the course of your year as a social chair. It is laid out on the assumption that you have been elected in November, but if your elections took place in May, you can skip to the second half of this chapter to get a sense of your initial priorities. This chapter also includes a discussion of the unique challenges, and opportunities, that come with holding parties in Texas in the summer.

NOVEMBER/DECEMBER

Good parties start with good planning. When you understand your priorities, you know what you should do next. When you don't, you don't. Here is a summary of the primary parties you'll work on during your spring semester, and what you need to be doing to make them crush.

First of all, don't allow your January party to drift until you come back to school. Deal with it straightaway. In reality, you will probably not be looking to book a giant national act for this party, because national acts don't book a month and a half out. If that *is* your intention, you'd better pick up the phone and start figuring out who's available the moment your budget is confirmed.

You'll probably be looking for a party band or a cover band. January is a dry time of year for those types of acts, which works to your advantage. A lot of the bands you'll be considering will either have come through a bookings drought in December or will be facing up to the post-Christmas blues. Very few people are booking or spending money in January. This is as true in the entertainment business as it is in retail.

A smart band knows that the opportunity to perform in the middle of January, especially if they're receiving notice in late November or early December, is an opportunity worth taking. This puts you in a position to lock in a band early, to save yourself from being stuck with that task when you get back to school, and to negotiate a better deal.

JANUARY

If you're back at school and you haven't finalized your January party, it's your top priority. Stop going to class if you need to, and turn your phone off. There is nothing more depressing, as a new social chair, to stand at a party you were responsible for quarterbacking and know that it's totally lame because you failed to organize any entertainment. This party will happen, and the only thing standing between you and humiliation at this point is your ability to throw it together on short notice.

On the other hand, a solid party sets the tone for the rest of your tenure. Getting the first one under your belt is a great feeling, and it gives you the confidence to succeed further.

Be responsible, and stay on top of your role. You've got multiple events to plan during the coming three months, and this is the time you need to start making decisions, even if you don't have all the information you want available to you.

Plan based upon what you know, and remember that a B+ party that happens is a *lot* better than an A+ party that doesn't happen. You can wait around forever on more information, but at some point you need to make some decisions.

Maybe you hear rumors that you have more money coming, or that your rival fraternity is planning something big. Beyond a certain point, that doesn't matter. If you have 80 percent of your budget firmed up, and you've identified a date that works for you, don't wait any longer. The reality is that, if you're the first to book a date, your competitors will need to either go head-to-head with you or work around you.

This is equally true if you're planning to work with another fraternity to put something big together, but they keep dragging their feet. It's important that you remain courteous and allow them time to bring their ideas and their money to the table, but if they're not doing so in a timely fashion, you need to let them go and take care of your own business.

FEBRUARY

By February, you should have an event under your belt. By this stage, you will have established budgets and dates. If you haven't confirmed the entertainment for your big spring event, you should at least have submitted a formal offer and be awaiting confirmation.

The time has come to execute your February party, which means making sure that your location is secure and ensuring that you have adequate production. Pretend that the event is happening tomorrow. Would it be a success? If not, what do you need to do to make it a success?

Put a spreadsheet together so you can see what needs to happen and when. Use it to create a checklist of the things you need to do, and act on that checklist. Past social chairs, if you have access to them, can be extremely helpful to you in determining what you need to focus on and what you may be forgetting. Perhaps they created a spreadsheet or some other form of record you can refer to.

What you're doing is not revolutionary. People have done this before, and the concepts of securing a venue, booking lighting and sound engineers, and hosting a show are very familiar. For that reason, it pays to ask the people who have done this before. There is no need to reinvent the wheel.

One of the biggest mistakes I see people make when they start booking a production team is thinking that they can step in if they have doubts about one of their vendors. Their production manager seems like an oddball, so they fire the guy. All of a sudden, they're the production manager, and they don't know what they're doing.

Another expression of this is thinking that your skills transfer to a much larger arena. Maybe you're a musician and you own a tiny PA and jam periodically with your friends. That's not going to prepare you to run a line array for a national act.

Always remember that you're not an expert, so unless you want to become one, and you're willing to do what it takes to make that happen within a few weeks, work it out with your production manager or find someone you *can* work with.

Production is an area best left to experts. It's good to be curious and to want to learn, but your job is to make sure your event goes well, and you have hundreds, perhaps thousands, of people expecting you to do that. Don't roll the dice on them.

The president of the United States is commander-in-chief of the army, but he doesn't walk his soldiers into battle. He delegates to generals. You need to follow that example and delegate the jobs you're not able to take on.

MARCH AND APRIL

The vast majority of fraternities hold their large spring parties in March and April. These are the culmination of the school year; the ideal time both to hold a blowout event and to give the next year's intake of fraternity brothers an idea of what the chapter is about.

For those reasons, it's crucial that spring parties are executed skillfully. You want to look good personally, and you also want your fraternity chapter to look good to potential new members.

To ensure that you have time to train your focus on the big spring party, you should have checked with your formal chair to ensure that you're not expected to handle the entertainment for your formal during the same time period. Most formal chairs will take care of booking a band, but they may request the benefit of your expertise because you have already built up much more experience than them. Additionally, you may have a parents' weekend or another small party to spearhead during this time.

These are minor concerns, however, in comparison with the outstanding possibilities of your main spring parties. In short, the six-week period between March and April is prime time.

To guarantee the success of these events, you will need to be very disciplined with your time. You have school, and you have other priorities, but unless you prefer to sub out, hire a company to do the heavy lifting for you, and watch from the sidelines, you will need to devote a significant portion of your time and attention to your responsibilities as social chair.

If your formal chair has asked you to book the band for a formal that falls in March or April, this should be done by now. Ideally, you want a party band, performing Motown classics or something similar, and providing their own small sound and lighting package.

Obviously, a self-contained act is far preferable for formals unless you have a turnkey company or a production company running these events on your behalf. There are a lot of moving parts you need to be aware of, and managing sound, lighting, and staging from a distance will only complicate your job unnecessarily.

The types of bands you will be looking to hire are very familiar with the process of coming into weddings and similar events, setting up, and playing with little input from you or the venue. Let them.

They should only need the basic schematics of the room and a connection with someone who can answer any questions they have pertaining to power and staging. Usually, these are best handled by connecting them with a representative of the venue.

March and April are peak wedding season, so if you haven't booked a band a couple of months ahead, you will probably need to go with whoever is available and pay a premium for the privilege.

For your big spring party, you should have confirmed your headliner long before now. If you haven't, you're way behind schedule, and it has to be your number-one priority. As long as you're set for a headliner, it's time to look at filling out the rest of the bill.

Your budget may have a big influence on how you approach this part of the planning. In a pinch, look locally. There will probably be a lot of people in your peer group who play in bands or who are aspiring DJs, and who would love the opportunity to perform in front of a large crowd.

Any creative professional knows that using the promise of "exposure" as payment is often a con, used in lieu of paying them properly. In principle, it's not something I want to encourage. That said, if you have a fraternity brother with a five-piece jam band that has only played a handful of shows, offering them the chance to warm up for a national or regional act, and play in front of thousands of people, may legitimately strike them as a great opportunity.

The same goes if you know a brother who is a sick rapper, or who has been sitting in his room all semester mixing beats and creating music on his laptop. Maybe this is the right time for him to get up in front of a crowd and show everyone what he's capable of. If you take the time to seek them out, you'll discover some amazingly talented people.

Adding a few warm-up acts to your bill can benefit everyone. Often, people won't show up early, and the last thing you want to do is put your headliner in front of a lackluster crowd. Your local openers will be happy, or at least happier, playing in front of twenty people. They probably need the practice, and they can trade off the credibility that comes from being on the bill at all.

Parents' weekend also takes place in March or April. The biggest trick to a successful parents' weekend is to think carefully about what will make your parents, and those of your peers, happy. Consider the median age of your year group's parents, and take a moment to figure out when they graduated. If you discover that the average parent graduated in 1987, think about what music they will enjoy. Find a band that really nails some Bon Jovi covers, and they'll be in heaven.

In Texas and the southeast, you can expect a boatload of classics such as "Brown Eyed Girl" and "Margaritaville," but if you can tailor the set list to the likely tastes of your parents, and the parents of your friends, that's a huge win. Make your parents happy, and give them a good feeling knowing that their money is going to a great school and that you're part of a great chapter. They're probably helping you with your tuition; the least you can do is give them a great night out and let them relive their youth for a few hours.

I first noticed this trend at a wedding, with a really skilled band that could cover anything. They broke into Bon Jovi's "Wanted Dead or Alive," from *Slippery When Wet*, and the crowd went absolutely wild. They were singing every word and having an amazing time.

I asked myself what was going on, and I realized that the mother of the bride graduated around the time *Slippery When Wet* came out.

It's so easy to get stuck in a routine of the same thirty songs when playing for parents' weekend. They're played again and again because they work, but they can become tired. Take the opportunity to play to your crowd, and give them an experience that they may not have been expecting and that they'll love.

MAY

Looking ahead to the fall, you can expect more events, but smaller budgets per event. You don't need each show to blow the roof off.

Nonetheless, the same rules apply. Even if all you want is for a band to come in for a tailgate at short notice, you still need to plan ahead, lock down your dates, and establish your budget. Be aware that the big teams you played away last year will probably be the ones you play at home this year.

Don't fret unnecessarily about dates, however. You know which games will be the biggest of the year, and you can create a hierarchy of events and allocate the budget accordingly, slotting them into the calendar as the schedule becomes clear.

This is the only time I'd recommend this approach. Tailgates are uncertain, and you're at the mercy of a calendar that you can't be totally clear on in advance. Plan as well as you can, and prepare to make moves as soon as you have dates in place.

Your biggest obstacle will be the long summer vacation. People won't be around to give you feedback or help you estimate your budget. Maybe you'll be away, too. You need to make plans as soon as possible, so that you can use the summer months productively.

Although you may not have dues in hand, it's reasonable to expect that they will be available when you need them. Dues keep your fraternity afloat, so you can project a budget based on dues that haven't yet been collected. If possible, obviously you'll want to collect dues ahead of time so that you have cash to work with.

Consider offering members of your chapter an incentive, such as a price break, for paying early. As mentioned earlier, as soon as you confirm an act they will want a deposit, so it's well worth the time and effort to make sure you have it.

In short, be cognizant of your dues and the projected timing of their collection. There's no better time than today to start a conversation about when you can expect to have the money you need to pay deposits.

Planning ahead is equally effective in case you want to lock in a production company. A lot of them work festivals in the summer, but they'll probably be excited by the offer of a solid gig in the fall.

Confirm a date and provide them with a deposit, and you'll be able to negotiate a better deal than you would if you waited until the final week of August to make a play for their time. In August, every fraternity in the area will be scrambling to plan their events because they haven't been responsible over the summer. Wait until then, and the good production companies may not be available at any price. Best case scenario, you'll be bringing someone in from out of town, at an extra cost. As long as they're not working a festival on the weekend when you call them, a production company will be happy to hear from you in the summer. Call them on a Tuesday, secure their services, and feel smug when every other social chair on campus is running around like a headless chicken in September.

SUMMER IN TEXAS

Unless you're in Texas, June, July, and early August are

wastelands for actual events. Texans, however, really take the opportunity to step up their game during the long vacation, and they have some truly amazing parties.

Often these are handled by rush chairs, in which case you may not be directly involved. They will want to create a great first impression for potential new members of the fraternity, and you may want to deploy your skills to help them. Overall, the plan of campaign for these events is very similar to the plan for producing spring parties in other areas.

The main priorities if you're in Texas and elected in May are similar to the priorities of someone elected in November, but the first big test comes in June or July. You, or your rush chair, have three months, or even less, to execute, meaning you don't have a lot of time to plan in advance.

Even if you're not in Texas, however, you may want to put on extracurricular summer parties. A sweet hack is to target bands that are playing festivals in your area. There are more festivals nowadays than ever before, and they're usually very strict at enforcing radius clauses.

What's a radius clause? It's an agreement that prevents bands from playing within a certain distance of an event within a certain timeline. Every band in history playing a festival wants to perform en route, making extra money and justifying the time they spend on the road.

The festival organizers, on the other hand, don't want them to play other gigs nearby, devaluing their presence at the festival.

Private parties, however, which these fraternity parties are, can provide an excellent loophole. They are not announced, formally promoted, or ticketed, meaning that bands can often perform at them without placing themselves in breach of contract.

Some festivals insist upon very, very strict radius clauses, which forbid even private performances, but they're usually more forgiving to fraternity parties than ticketed gigs. In some cases, it may even be possible for bands to perform under an alias, if you promise not to advertise their presence.

If you're planning an event and you like the idea of booking a band that will be passing through your town on the way to or from a festival, start looking at festivals within about a three-hundred-mile radius of your school. Alternatively, check to see if performers have to pass near your school to get where they're going.

An excellent example is Bonnaroo. If you know that a band living in New Orleans has to be in Manchester, Tennessee, for Bonnaroo, and your school is in Tuscaloosa, Alabama, you can calculate that there's a high probability they'll be driving through your area before or after the festival.

Similarly, if there's a big event in Suwannee, Florida, you're at the University of Georgia, and a band you want to see is coming down from North Carolina or New York, it's highly likely they'll be passing through the Athens and Atlanta area.

Reach out to them and propose a deal to get them on stage. You're in a good position, because they'll be happy to make some money on the way to their festival appearance. It's also probable that you won't be competing against a lot of other offers, because the radius clause will prevent that.

You can make your summer very fun and interesting, simply by looking up the festivals near you, checking out some of the smaller names on the ticket, and reaching out to them to see what will work.

Even if you're not planning to curate any parties over the summer, you can use the time as a great opportunity to research future bookings. Go to some festivals, listen to some live music, and work up a short list of great acts.

You've been elected as a social chair either because you have a reputation for having great taste or because your fraternity brothers think you're disciplined and organized. If the former, you probably already go to a lot of gigs, so continue doing what you're doing. If the latter, take some tastemakers with you to a few festivals, and get their opinions.

The bands you want to target are the ones in the small print toward the bottom of the bill. The headliners will be out of your league, but the small bands, that have made it on to the daytime slots, probably have a lot going for them.

The simple fact that they are on the bill at all indicates that they have good backing and a good agent and manager. They may have a record label backing them. With all those pieces in place, there's a high chance that they'll grow and become more popular.

They may catch a break as a result of playing at the very festival where you're watching them. It happens all the time. A band plays a killer set and finds their way onto the Instagram feed of someone influential, and before you know it they're blowing up. Keep tabs on the bands you like, and you may be able to book an act that you'll look back on one day and think: "Holy shit, they played at our fraternity house."

Another advantage of researching bands at festivals is that you're seeing them in a live setting. Most festivals don't use sound checks. They employ what's known as a line check. Essentially, this means that bands arrive, plug in, adjust their sound levels, and start to play. Adjustments are made on the fly.

It's a far cry from a traditional sound check, where bands show up hours before their set and fine-tune their sound so that when they come out to perform it's perfect. Festivals simply don't have the luxury of that kind of time. They're dealing with a high volume of entertainers, and those acts need to be on their toes.

This means that, when you see an up-and-coming band at a festival, you're getting a very solid sample of what they can produce at your fraternity house. You can tell how well rehearsed they are, and how tight their sound is. It's a very good advertisement for a potential gig at a big party later in the year.

If you're not stacked with events to plan in the summer, have some fun and do some research by going to some festivals. This is a great opportunity to see which bands are coming down the pipe and to hear them live. It's a lot easier to pitch an act to the rest of your chapter when you can say that you've seen them perform and they absolutely nailed it. In the case that you're not considered an arbiter of what's cool, taking a tastemaker with you will also mean that he can vouch for you and head off resistance at the pass.

SEPTEMBER

By the time you're back at school, your September party should be planned and almost ready to roll. If it's not, you had better skip class, quit your job, and do whatever it takes to make it happen, including delegating anything you can to others to maximize your efficiency. Time is of the essence.

You need to look at your calendar, establish your budget, and prioritize based upon the largest acts you want to book. The largest bands will require the greatest lead time, so once you've decided whom you want to book, don't delay a moment longer than necessary before taking action.

If you've been holding off on offers because you've been waiting on dues, you can't wait much longer. Parties will be coming thick and fast, and if you don't move fast, you'll be left behind.

In March and April, bands are in demand because it's wedding season. In September, October, and November, bands are in demand because there are so many fraternities and sororities competing for the same few bands over the same short period of time. If you're looking to book a local favorite, you can rest assured that you'll find yourself embroiled in a bidding war, whether you realize it or not.

This is especially true with Halloween parties. You probably have a choice of two different nights or, at most, two different weekends. This will drive up demand for certain bands and create a competitive atmosphere between you and your peers.

OCTOBER

October is football season, so you can expect to be executing tailgates. Not all tailgates are created equal. Before the season starts, rank them and put the greatest effort into the biggest one. The smaller ones can be handled much closer to the date they take place. Look for a big rivalry, when you know you'll have friends from other schools and family members, for an opportunity to blow one up.

The best way to make sure that you have a large enough budget available, while also retaining the flexibility to change plans if necessary, is to work out a combined budget for the entire tailgate season.

A lot of people do this, and then they arbitrarily apply numbers to individual events. They might allocate $2,000 to some of the tailgates, $3,000 to others, and maybe $5,000 to the biggest.

They're thinking in the right way but missing the chance to execute something special. Let's say you have a $20,000 budget for all the tailgates combined. With the caveat that you don't want to spend more than 50 percent of the total budget on a single event, take that budget and do what it takes to execute your biggest tailgate.

If you have $12,000 left, go and execute the next largest tailgate, again making sure you don't spend more than 50 percent of the remaining budget.

If you only spend $1,500 on the lowest-priority tailgates, no one will mind, because they know that the rest of the budget has gone on some serious parties for the biggest tailgates. Alternatively, you can simply drop one or two from the schedule. You can adapt easily to small changes. What you can't do is bring in a headliner at short notice, with an ill-defined budget.

I think prioritizing your most important tailgates and budgeting accordingly is the most effective path. People remember the events that really blow them out of the water. Knock their socks off once or twice, and you'll secure your reputation as a great social chair far more effectively than you would with four or five average parties.

Ideally, you've made inquiries and you have a headliner

expecting your call. When you have the tailgate schedule, go back to them, or their agent, and tell them when the big one is happening. Next, talk to your production crew and let them know that they can expect one thousand people at this one, as opposed to 120 or 150.

If you don't do this, your production guys may turn up with a moderate rig that is fine for up to two hundred people but inadequate for a big band and one thousand people. You'll be in double jeopardy. Your artist won't be happy, and you will have wasted money booking them without making them sound good.

You may want to bring in self-contained bands for the smaller tailgates. This is a win-win. Your production crew will be happy knowing that they made out on your larger events. They'd much rather make $2,000 from one big party than come back week after week for $300, exposing their gear to the risk of theft or damage.

October is also go time for your Halloween party. Halloween parties are some of the most competitive events of the year. Whatever you're planning, you can bet that there's another fraternity, or a sorority, with a similar idea.

Virtually every Halloween party will take place either on the Friday or the Saturday directly before Halloween, so if you're looking for a national act, you will be competing not only with other fraternities at your school but also with other schools in your vicinity.

Just as in the summer, consider seeking out bands that may be passing through your area to or from a fall festival. You may be able to negotiate a more competitive price without triggering a radius clause and also beat other fraternities to the punch by being smart and taking a route they haven't considered.

Think back to last year's party, and if necessary consult the people who organized it. Did anything go wrong? Perhaps you had a great DJ with a sick light show, but the haze triggered the fire alarm, and he only got two-thirds of the way through his set before the fire truck arrived and you had to evacuate the house.

You can't legally disconnect the fire alarm, but you can take the DJ outside or adjust the show so that it doesn't require fog or haze to look cool.

For a Halloween party, the chances are that you're looking at one major act with a local band or a DJ in support. Unlike a spring party, where you may have three or four larger acts and you can afford to let one walk if they give you trouble, this will leave you highly leveraged on ensuring that the show proceeds smoothly and that your headlining band or DJ is happy.

Talk with your production crew beforehand, and ask their opinions. They may have crucial insights for you. For example, you may not realize that a particular room has terrible acoustics because the walls are made of concrete blocks, but the people who attend your party will know soon enough when they leave with their heads ringing, or when they stay outside socializing because it's less painful than being inside listening to the band.

Some styles of music work better in certain environments, and the best people to tell you are the guys on production.

Always keep a worst-case scenario in mind, so that you can plan for it. What would you do if the fire alarm went off? Could people exit the house in an orderly fashion, without anyone getting hurt? If you're planning an outside party, how likely is it that neighbors will be upset by the noise and call the police?

Taking a party outside can solve some problems, but it can also create others. Maybe there was a reason the party was held inside last year. Maybe there's a little old lady next door who will be on the phone to the cops the minute she hears a beat. Imagine everything that can go wrong, and you'll be well prepared to make everything go right.

NOVEMBER

November is a chill time of year. You may be called upon to put together a semiformal, which usually involves bringing in a party band such as a Motown band.

Feel free to go against the grain if you trust your taste and your audience, however. Perhaps you know a band that plays original songs, but who are comfortable peppering their set with covers. Maybe you know a performer who mainly plays covers but who gives the guitar solos an extra rip.

Semiformals are a great opportunity to bring in a variation on more formal party bands, because they are essentially date nights. They're also the perfect partners for parents' weekends when you're looking to book a band for two gigs at once and save some money.

Most semiformals take place outside fraternity houses, so make sure you have access to the venue. This is another reason to choose a self-contained band. It's difficult to prepare adequate production and lighting when you don't know the venue. An exception to this comes if you're working with a production company, a turnkey company, or a venue that provides in-house production. They will be able to scope out the schematics of the venue and handle the lighting and production for you.

A YEAR OF PARTIES

By the time you reach the end of your tenure as social chair, you will have presided over many parties. Whether you took on the role because you want to work in event management, or purely because you like to rage, you'll have developed an enormous amount of experience that your successor can benefit from.

Giving useful advice to whoever comes after you is both the gentlemanly thing to do and an enormous service to your chapter. You want to keep going to great parties, and the best way to do that is to make sure the next social chair has the information he needs to make a success of his role.

If you had this experience yourself, you'll understand how valuable it is. If you didn't, you'll understand how helpful it would have been. This is your opportunity to break new ground and change the way things are done.

Of course, it's the new social chair's job to keep an open mind and listen to your advice. You can't force anyone to benefit from your wisdom. If he has any sense, he will appreciate what you've already done and want to build on your work, recognizing that he can learn a lot from you.

Often, you'll know who will succeed you a month or so prior to the actual election. He may run unopposed, or the election itself may be nothing more than a formality. Show him the ropes, and let him know you're available when he needs some support.

ORDER OF OPERATIONS

—

Good job. You've checked out the calendar, and you understand what you need to focus on first. Now you need to start delivering. Whatever your starting date may be, you'll be in post for a year, and you have a lot of parties to spearhead.

The key players here are you, your president, and your treasurer. Everybody has a different perspective. Like you, your president probably wants to see a gigantic event come off, generating publicity and social capital for your chapter. You want the same thing, but you also want the personal kudos that comes with being the guy in charge of the kickass party.

You and the president will see eye to eye on many things. The treasurer, on the other hand, has a bird's eye view of the chapter's finances. He wants to see you succeed, and he likes to party, but his priorities are different. He knows that you are only one of many people who will be asking him for money. He should, therefore, be much more of a stickler about the budget than you or the president. Be thankful for this. If he's not, he's probably not a good treasurer.

Your role is equivalent to being the CEO of a company. You're the visionary here. It's your job to find creative ways of achieving the goals of your "business" (i.e., your fraternity). Your president is the equivalent of the company president. He is the figurehead of the fraternity as a whole, but he's not as directly involved in the process as you are. Your treasurer, naturally, is equivalent to the CFO, who holds the purse strings.

You were elected to your position because people believe in your ability to spot talent and create an amazing party. Your president is the face of the fraternity. He's on your side, but you can't count on him to bail you out if you mess up. Your treasurer may be a bit nerdier and less engaged with the overall vision, but he's doing an essential service by preventing you from going over budget.

It's absolutely vital that all three of you are involved in the process of establishing budgets.

KNOW YOUR BUDGET

Whether you've been elected in November or May, you have a vacation coming up and a party on the other side of it. What is the most effective use of your time?

Right now, you have access to the people who can provide you with the feedback you need, whether that's an opinion on the nature of the party, an accurate picture of how much you have to spend, or an idea of when other fraternities are planning events.

Your important tastemakers, your treasurer, and other social chairs are all still in town. They haven't left to go skiing or visit Grandma. That situation will change soon, so you'd better make the most of it.

In addition to your responsibilities as social chair, you need to study and prepare for your own vacation, so timing is of the essence. Once the people you need have left town, the chances of their responding to calls, emails, and text messages in a timely fashion are slim.

Beyond a shadow of a doubt, your first step should be to connect with your treasurer and ask him for a realistic assessment of your budget. Without an understanding of your buying power, any moves you make to book bands or secure venues may turn out to be an exercise in futility.

If you don't know your budget, figure out *why* you don't know it, and *when* you will. This may involve a serious discussion with your treasurer.

Are you expecting additional funds from alumni? Is your house or chapter subject to a nonannual expense such as a new roof? Your treasurer should have his eye on the bigger picture here and let you know how much you can allocate to parties.

Your budget gives you a clear idea of what you can expect to accomplish. On the positive side, that could mean building up a war chest, because your fraternity has been on probation for six months and the funds have been stacking up. In this case, you'll probably know all about it because of the buzz around the fraternity about the sick party you'll be able to throw when you're released from probation.

If the roof needs to be replaced or the parking lot needs repaving, however, it's much less likely that you'll be aware of it. This is why it's important to do some digging and ascertain your buying power.

There's no sense wasting your time and energy looking for $20,000 acts when you only have $10,000 to spend. That's just spinning your wheels. Get a healthy understanding of your budget, and make sure that it's in writing so that you can reference it later.

Ideally, get an email from your treasurer, and get him to copy it to your president. It's too easy to catch your treasurer at a bad time, while his mind is in seven different places, and discover later on that he's given you flawed information. Having it in writing prevents this.

Always request a conservative budget. Even treasurers, who have been elected for their perceived fiscal responsibility, can be prone to exaggeration. Remember, you can always, always add money to a budget. Never, in the whole history of the human race, has discovering additional funds created a problem.

Finding that there's a shortfall in the budget, after you've already made commitments to acts, agents, and production guys, however, can get you into a lot of trouble. If this happens, things can get hairy very quickly.

In the worst case scenario, you may find yourself writing checks that you can't cash. A minor and more likely problem is that you will waste time researching acts and venues that aren't available to you. You're a busy person. Don't waste your time.

What happens if you can't establish a working budget? Perhaps you haven't collected dues, or it's still unclear whether the fraternity house will need a new roof. Maybe there are rumors of alumni donating money to the chapter, but you haven't seen any sign of cold, hard cash yet.

In that case, your starting point is to look backward. How much did your chapter spend last year? How were the parties? Did the previous social chair put the chapter's money to good use? If not, why not, and what could you do better? Do you need to spend less money on the biggest party of the year, in order to free up funds for other parties? Alternatively, do you need to allocate more money to a single party and turn it into a massive blowout?

Talk to your previous social chair, and particularly to your former treasurer. A good treasurer can bring boatloads of insight to your process.

Once you've determined a budget for the semester, rank your events in order of importance.

If your spring event is the biggest of the year, place it at the top of the list. If you're planning to bring in a national act for your February party, put it second. Maybe you or one of your fraternity brothers has parents who are about to donate $3 million to build a new fraternity house. In that case, you'd better make parents' weekend your next priority.

Alternatively, if you've been elected in May and you're determined to throw a Halloween party that blows everyone else out of the water, rank that at the top of your priorities.

Once you've sketched out your total budget and your priorities, you can begin to allocate funds. Don't spend money on anything you don't need to spend money on. If a $2,000 party band will get the job done, hire them. Don't choose a $5,000 band unless they will be significantly better.

That $3,000 could enable you to book the DJ you want for your big spring event. It could pay for a nicer lighting rig and a bigger band at your parents' weekend. Be methodical with your spending. Don't apply arbitrary budgets purely because you have money to spend and you think it might as well go somewhere.

One of the most common situations I encounter when working with social chairs is coming in and discovering that they have budgets laid out that make little to no sense. I ask them how they've chosen those figures, and they say: "I don't know. It just seemed right."

Thinking carefully about your budgets before you get started will allow you to track your spending and decide whether you're really making the best use of your money. This also creates an opportunity to reallocate funding to other events if you find that you have a surplus.

Formals sometimes have their own separate budget, as do parents' weekends. It's not always possible to mix and match. Nonetheless, be efficient. Make good use of the money placed in your trust.

It's easy to sit down with your treasurer and decide that you have $20,000 allocated to your big spring event. Perhaps there's a good reason for that. Maybe that's been the budget for the past six years, and it's seen as a magic number that allows you to book a great band and drive home the message that your fraternity knows how to party, while still leaving enough on the table to throw solid parties for the rest of the spring semester.

Alternatively, that budget could be totally arbitrary. Perhaps no one has ever thought to question the amount. Could you shave $5,000 from the rest of the semester's events and do something bigger? Is the inverse true? Could you shave $5,000 from the spring party budget and still host an equally amazing event?

A lot of bigger fraternities have built up a brand that attracts people regardless of who is performing. They can afford to subtract some money from the budget of their biggest party without losing momentum, and redirect those funds to the creation of a new event.

You want to spend the money available to you as efficiently as possible, maximizing the quality of the experience for everyone involved. To do this, you'll need to do more than glance quickly at a budget sheet. Sit down with your treasurer shortly after your election, think critically, and work out a budget that gets you excited about the parties you can pull off, while still being conservative enough to satisfy his most miserly tendencies.

Take budgeting seriously. It's easy to count on money that may or may not materialize, and potentially get yourself into big trouble through booking a band you can't afford.

If your chapter collects dues on January 15, you know that you will be able to pay a deposit on January 16. That's an understanding based on fact. If dues aren't collected, there will be much bigger problems afoot than your party.

If you heard some of the alumni are going to kick in some extra money so you can have an outrageous party this spring, you have no idea whether that will actually happen. When it's in the bank, it's real. Until then, you need to operate on the principle that you don't have it. It's great, in theory, but you have parties to plan. Tell them to show you the money. When they do, you can increase the budget.

Perhaps you've been told that your chapter is planning to

consolidate events, meaning that you will be responsible for fewer parties, and each one will have a bigger budget. In that case, get the information in writing and make sure that your president and your treasurer are copied into the email. Always know your budget, and protect yourself by only counting on funds that already exist or are guaranteed.

CHOOSE YOUR DATES

Once you have established your total budget, your next step is to lock down dates for your major events. There are numerous factors that will determine your choice, not least the fact that there are a limited number of weekends around the times you're looking to host your parties, and there are lots of other fraternities planning parties around the same time. This is especially true of big spring events.

Do you want to compete with your biggest rival and split their audience? Do you want to battle it out with another fraternity for the same act? What if they have greater buying power than you? Are you determined to set trends, or are you willing to follow them?

Whatever your scenario, there are ways to win, but be aware of who else is planning a party around the same time as you, and how that may affect your choice of date. Find out who the big dogs are, and don't square off directly against them. There's no sense in competing against the biggest party of the spring season, so choose another weekend.

Be willing to work with people to ensure that everyone's event is successful. There are only a limited number of weekends available, so it may be impossible to avoid a clash with another fraternity. Maybe one can have a day party that winds up around dusk, while the other gets going at sunset and rolls on late into the night.

Sometimes it's difficult to get ahold of the information you need. In that case, perhaps your best move is simply to choose a date and let everyone else work around it. This can be highly effective if you're a big fish, or word gets out that you're planning to go big with your entertainment. If that's not the case, however, you can still make this approach work to your advantage by going early. Hold your big spring event in late March, and usher in the season.

There are lots of ways to be successful. You don't have to have the most money, and you don't have to have the greatest clout, but you do need to be intentional in your planning, know your buying power, and develop a clear idea of your timing.

THIS IS A REPUBLIC, NOT A DEMOCRACY

It's time to start researching bands. The way to do this is emphatically *not* to walk around the fraternity asking people what they think would be cool. This will give you no positive information and will be a complete waste of your time.

You were elected because you know more than the average partygoer. Their opinions matter, and they're an important part of the fraternity. For the purposes of organizing a party, however, they don't know what they're talking about. Don't treat them as though they do.

If you must, give them the illusion of choice by offering up some suggestions and requesting their feedback, but don't simply throw open the question of which bands to book to them. It will not benefit your decision-making process in any way. In all likelihood, their suggestions will be totally unrealistic, and you will have achieved nothing more valuable than raising their expectations to a level you can't possibly satisfy.

A much better approach is to find three to five people in your fraternity whose opinions you trust and respect. They will be your tastemakers. Possibly you were elected not because you have the best taste in music but because you're a disciplined and organized leader. If so, that's for the best. The guy who goes to all the shows and hangs out backstage is a fan boy, not a leader. He would make a terrible social chair, but he may have some great recommendations for you.

As a social chair, you don't need to have all the answers, but you do need to have access to the people who do. Reach out to the three to five people whose opinions you value and ask for their feedback. Let them reach out to three to five people whose opinions *they* value. The information you get from this process will be a hundred times more valuable than any information you can glean from asking your fraternity brothers en masse.

If necessary, present your tastemakers with specific questions. Do they want a rapper, a DJ, or a band? Let's say they suggest booking a band. Ask them to bring you the names of three bands that they think would be good choices.

It's highly likely that you'll notice patterns. The same bands' names will come up more than once. At this point, you can compile a list of your top three options, go back to your tastemakers once more, and ask them what they think. They probably won't even need to go back to their contacts again to let you know whether you've got a good read on the preferences of the chapter.

Remember, you're still the leader here, and you have veto power. You're doing your contacts a favor by giving them an opportunity to be involved in the process of creating the chapter's parties. At the same time, you're increasing the chances of making a good, informed decision. If you don't like their suggestions, you can rule them out.

Think of the process of gleaning feedback as the equivalent of being the president of the United States and requesting advice from your most trusted experts and advisers.

You wouldn't send out an email blast to three hundred million people asking them to give you their best ideas about health-care reform. If you did that, you wouldn't be able to go through all the data. There would be too much. Probably 98 percent of it would be garbage; and, worse, there would be a very good chance that any good ideas would be overlooked in the mountain of nonsense.

In the best case scenario, issuing a general invitation to give you feedback will result in your receiving worthless information. In a worst case scenario, you'll receive worthless information, waste a lot of time, and promote discontent in the ranks. People will suggest a $200,000 rapper who was never, at any point, a possibility. Then, when you have to tell them that isn't happening, they'll be upset and feel as if their voices aren't being heard.

In short, nothing good can come out of asking the masses for suggestions.

SMART BOOKING STRATEGIES

Always look to bundle bands together for better value. This can apply to a single event, if you're having a big spring party that will feature multiple bands, or it can apply to several events, if you're having three parties that require the same level of talent.

Agents may play hardball with you, but the reality is that if you reach out to one and tell him or her that you have multiple events, or multiple slots at the same event, then you're in a good position to negotiate a better deal.

In the simplest terms, you're offering the agent the opportunity to make three commissions from sending one email, as opposed to three commissions over the course of many, many interactions over a period of months. Who wouldn't be interested in that deal?

It's a highly efficient way to work, and it represents a win-win for both you and the agent. Naturally, however, it's only effective if you're interested in booking an artist several times, or if the agent you're working with represents more than one artist you want to book.

This is where getting middle buyers involved can be a smart call. They have the flexibility to approach any artist, whereas agents who work for a company that represents a specific roster are bound to that roster.

Wal-Mart succeeds by employing economies of scale to buy products in volume. You're obviously not going to match Wal-Mart's buying power, but you can use the same principle.

If an agent tells you that a band usually books for $3,000 to $4,000, try offering $2,750 per show to book two shows, and tell him you're willing to pay the deposit on both immediately. The worst case scenario is that he says no.

Remember, too, that these are informal conversations. You're not yet at the stage of putting in a formal offer. You're exploring your options, as you should. You'll want to have similar conversations with the production crew, the lighting guy, the sound guy, the stage guy, and anyone else you're looking to hire. If you find a competent sound guy whom you like working with, offer him the chance to work on all your fall events in exchange for a discount.

Be careful not to enter into an agreement with someone whose work sucks. Make sure that they know what they're doing first.

Nonetheless, bundling is an excellent tactic. Most people will be willing to make a deal if they know they're going to secure a contract to work multiple events. That's a good reason for them to give you a better price.

There's an art to negotiating the best possible deals, and we'll cover it in much greater depth in part two of this book.

A warning before we move on, however. You have been elected to this position. It is your responsibility. It is *never* permissible for any nonelected member of your chapter to make moves on any entertainment or production without your consent.

If you discover that this is happening, it is your job to squash it immediately. In a scenario where that person has the backing of you treasurer or president, it is imperative that you have strong words with your treasurer or president immediately.

Too many cooks in the kitchen screw up the casserole, and nothing will undermine your efforts faster than having a rogue member of your chapter running around showing your cards to prospective agents and vendors.

In a situation where there are multiple people speaking on behalf of the client, the only person who wins is the vendor. Don't allow yourself to be backed into this position.

TALKING TO PRODUCTION ENGINEERS

Whom do you need to talk to about lighting and sound, and what should you say to them?

If you're using a production company, reach out to them early. The first thing you will want to ask them is how much they charge for their services. The first question they will ask you is: "What's your budget?"

They won't want to tell you how much they charge, because they want to know your budget. You won't want to tell them your budget, because you want to know how much they charge. That's how it goes.

They don't want to explain what every nut and bolt costs and what it does. They want some parameters so they can give you ballpark figures. Meanwhile, you don't want to reveal every aspect of your budget, because you don't want them to screw you for everything you've got. If you want anything to get done, everyone involved will need to be a little flexible.

The reason it's important to start talking to these people as soon as possible is that they are essential to executing your event. It doesn't matter if you have the biggest band in the country booked; without production, they're nothing but eye candy, at least until people start getting mad and throwing things at them.

Again, it's a good idea to talk to them about multiple events and get them on the hook early. The world of production is a feast or famine environment. Reach out to them during a time of scarcity, when they're worried about how they're going to eat next month, and they will be highly receptive to you. On the other hand, if you're trying to get a hold of them when they're slammed to the gills, they probably won't even return your call.

You can make serious savings by approaching engineers early. Even if they're a highly in-demand company and they don't give you a big discount, you can get the peace of mind that comes with knowing that you're covered, and you won't be scrambling around looking for production closer to the time of the event, which can be nerve-racking and add to your costs.

Local companies often do great work, but they may only have a limited quantity of gear, meaning they won't be able to handle multiple events on the same day. If you're late to the party, you may be forced to engage a company from out of town and add their travel costs to your bill. The sooner you begin talking to your engineers, the greater your chances are of finding a quality company at a good price.

BOOK THE BIGGEST NAMES FIRST

Just as you need to prioritize certain events, so also you

need to prioritize the most important *aspects* of each event. Larger entertainers will always require more lead time than smaller bands. They're more sought after, and they book three to six months in advance as opposed to one or two months.

Don't worry about the opening regional act. In all likelihood, they will be excited to perform because they know that they'll be opening for a national act, and making enough money to pay off the debt on their van.

The guy that won't be so excited is the headliner that you want to book who has fifteen other offers to consider. Make him your priority, and then work backward. Move from event to event.

For example, imagine that you've just succeeded in booking a national act for your big spring party. Don't shift your focus directly to booking a support act. That can wait. Book the headliner for your second most important party, probably your February event.

Booking big-name artists should always be at the top of your to-do list, because of the time lag and the difficulty in replacing them at short notice. This also works to your advantage because, when you secure the big guy, the little guys will come out of the woodwork. They may start calling you.

You don't need to organize an entire event before moving on to the next. In some contexts, that's a good principle, but not in this one. You have many projects to handle simultaneously, and it's imperative that you take a bird's eye view and allocate your time, energy, and money where it is most needed at any given moment.

THE BIGGEST MISTAKES

New social chairs always want to spend as much of their budget as possible on entertainment. That's where they think they will see the biggest return on their investment, whether they count those returns in cool points, number of attendees, personal satisfaction, or chapter bragging rights.

The trouble is, this often means neglecting production.

No one cares about production until it isn't there, at which point it becomes a disaster. The single biggest mistake I see social chairs making, day in and day out, is spending a disproportionate amount of money on entertainment and too little on production.

This makes even great acts look mediocre. If you put the Rolling Stones onto a beat-up wooden stage with no lights, they will look like a bunch of geriatrics. The success of your party is dependent on making the acts you've booked look and sound larger than life.

If you fail to do this, it doesn't matter how talented they are. They will not look and sound as good as they should. If they even agree to play, you will have spent a disproportionate percentage of your budget on talent that isn't being showcased as well as it could be. At the same time, you will have attracted a large crowd of people to a party they thought was going to be epic, only to disappoint them and lose their trust.

Balancing how much you spend on production and staging is a very tricky job, and finding the balance comes primarily with experience. It's vitally important that you have enough production, but you don't want to waste money on power and lights that you won't get value from. When you're starting out, you may need to rely heavily on those who have done the job before you.

Don't book a band and assume that everything will work out. I've seen this happen many, many times. Social chairs book the talent and then apply an arbitrary budget to production based on an entirely inaccurate estimate of how much they think it will cost.

Remember that, for an average spring party, you're asking people to spend six hours loading in $50,000 worth of equipment, to work a ten-hour day, and then to spend another four hours packing up the same equipment. How much could that possibly cost? No more than $1,500, right? Wrong.

You need to know in advance how much production will cost you, so that you can make an informed decision about how much of your budget can be directed toward the entertainment. Too often, social chairs neglect this step entirely, with the result that they either go well over budget or they serve up subpar entertainment.

Work out how big a slice of your budget needs to go toward production before you start speaking to agents. If your total budget is $20,000, and you tell an agent that, he or she will try to sell you acts that cost $20,000. It's the agents' job to get as much money as possible for their clients.

This is a great reason to work with a skilled middle buyer and ask her to negotiate on your behalf. The reality is that you don't have much experience in this role, and you're at high risk of being stiffed. Nonetheless, you can reduce your headaches by working out your production costs before you speak to an agent, and giving her a budget based on what she really needs to know, which is how much you're willing to spend booking one of her artists.

In the scenario above, you probably need to allocate between $4,000 and $5,000 on production costs if you're holding your event outside, and $2,000 to 3,000 if it's inside. Setting up lighting and sound outdoors is a more expensive endeavor than doing it in a more confined, indoor space.

The best way to get an estimate is to talk to your sound guys. Tell them how many people you anticipate having at your event, the venue, and approximately how long it will last. Ask them for a ballpark figure to run the event. They'll undoubtedly be cautious about giving you an exact number, but they'll probably be willing to give you something you can take to the table when you're speaking to an agent.

Now you're informed. When an agent asks you what your budget is, lowball it slightly. For an outdoor event, tell him that it will probably be in the range of $14,000 to $15,000.

At this point, the conversation can take many different turns, which will be discussed in greater depth in part three. The principle, however, is that by building in your production costs and not showing your hand straightaway, you give yourself some room to maneuver.

If the agent tells you the act you want books for $20,000, maybe you can move the show inside, free up a couple thousand dollars, and meet the agent halfway. You may even impress him when he realizes that you've taken the time to research production costs thoroughly. That's not a possibility if you reveal your entire budget from the beginning of the negotiation.

To compound the impression that you know what you're doing, and potentially save yourself a considerable amount of money, ask the agent to shoot you a tech rider. This is an easy request for an agent to fulfill. A tech rider usually comes in PDF form, and it details the band's technical requirements.

You probably won't understand it, but your sound engineer, lighting engineer, and stage technician will. Ask them what they think, and they'll tell you how much production will cost based on the rider.

They will also be able to identify any areas where the expense seems unnecessary and flag them for you. If a particular piece of equipment will raise your production costs from $2,000 to $4,500, a good sound guy will notice. You can take that information back to the agent and use it to have an informed discussion.

Another advantage of asking for a tech rider is that you will make an impression on the agent, purely by making the request.

Agents spend a lot of time speaking to people from fraternities. In many cases, the person they speak to isn't even the elected official, just some guy who's trying to do the chapter a solid. They get *very* bored of fielding bogus questions and inquiries based upon nothing more than a vague idea of what might be possible.

As soon as you ask an agent for a tech rider, so that you can get a clearer idea of how much you have to spend on his artist, he'll probably begin to think you have a brain, and that you have a realistic interest in booking his talent. He may even shoot you straight.

The second most common mistake I see is a failure to understand technical requirements. When you sign a contract that says you agree to all the requirements on the tech rider, you will be expected to meet those requirements.

If you haven't understood those requirements correctly, you run the risk of two different screw-ups. Either you hand them to your production guy and discover that they cost far more than you anticipated, or you ignore them and find that your artist arrives on the day of the show to inadequate production and simply walks away.

Should that happen, the artist will keep the deposit you gave them, and they will require you to pay them the outstanding balance. If you don't, they can sue you for breach of contract. Will they? Maybe not, but it's highly unlikely that they'll do business with you again any time soon. It hardly needs to be said that you do not want this to happen.

The third major mistake I encounter time and again is submitting more than one formal offer.

You're not an agent, and you're not experienced in booking talent. When you take on your role as social chair, you probably don't know what a formal offer is. Agents often take advantage of this by casually asking you to submit a formal offer and sending you a template you can use to do so. What you probably won't notice is the small print at the bottom that informs you that your formal offer is a legally binding contract, obliging you to pay the amount specified in the offer upon confirmation.

In other words, you don't have a get-out clause. You should only submit a formal offer when you are 100 percent certain that you're ready to book a band or artist, and you have the money available. If you submit more than one formal offer, and more than one artist agrees to your terms, you are legally obliged to pay them both. Don't let an agent sucker you into submitting a formal offer before you're ready.

Agents aren't necessarily out to fleece you, although some are. They do, however, deal with a lot of bullshit. They field a lot of calls from people who are shopping around and aren't serious about booking their acts. Asking you to submit a formal offer allows them to instantly know whether you're genuinely interested in their services or merely kicking tires.

Telling them, politely but firmly, that you're not ready to submit a formal offer and that you're exploring several options lets them know both that you're informed of proper protocol and that you won't be strong-armed into doing something you're not comfortable with. It also lets the agent know where you stand, and it should inspire him to work harder for your business.

JOINT PARTIES

Joint parties are an outstanding way to capitalize on collective resources, boosting both your budget and your expected attendance. You can do much more in a group than you can do alone. They can be truly amazing events.

Be aware, however, that each additional stakeholder creates more moving parts and makes execution harder and more complex. If you find it hard to get things done in your own chapter, your job will be two or three times as hard when you need to take into account the preferences of several more people.

More opinions create more lag time. Make sure that the people you bring to the table are on the same page as you with regard to your vision for the event. Resolving conflicts becomes progressively more difficult the further into the process you get. If you love jam bands, and your partner fraternity wants to bring in a rapper, that's not a good fit.

By the same token, don't partner with a fraternity that you know doesn't have a lot of money, or you don't trust to produce the money in a timely fashion. Ask yourself whether your prospective partners will really be assets to the operation. If not, don't work with them.

Indecision is a decision. Working with indecisive people will only bring you down and harm your event. In parties, as in life, don't allow others to bring you down.

In addition, you may discover that as soon as you start laying the groundwork for an event, the indecisive partners magically start to get their act together. Seeing you making moves can be a great catalyst to spur them into action.

Money talks. If you have $10,000 to spend on a joint party with a sorority, another local fraternity, or a chapter of your brothers from a neighboring school, in theory that's a $20,000 show. Until they've ponied up the money, however, what you really have is a $10,000 party.

You know an event is going to happen. So, instead of waiting on them indefinitely, go ahead and secure the production you need. Explore options that fit your budget.

Naturally, the choices available to you on a $10,000 budget will be less glorious than those available to you on a $20,000 budget, but you're operating within your sphere of influence. It's up to you to decide that you *will* have a party, and it *will* be good. If it's not as big as it could be, that won't be your fault. It'll be the fault of the chapter that wasted your time and failed to deliver.

The best part of operating like this is that, if your energy and decisiveness inspires them and they choose to get on board, you will have already covered your bases with regard to production. The extra $10,000 they bring to the party can be applied directly to hiring entertainment that blows the roof off.

If that's your scenario, you can move the original act that you booked when you thought your total budget was $10,000 to the opening slot on your bill. Now you have a two-band bill. You won't be able to book as big an act as you would have done if your partners had brought their money to the table earlier, but you will be doing everything you can to have the best party you can have, and making the most of the available information and finances at your disposal.

Remember always that your loyalty is to putting on a great show. If another fraternity house enters into a verbal agreement, or even a written agreement, to collaborate with you on a party, that means nothing until they have money on the table.

If they break a contract, you can spend two years suing them, and you'll probably win, but that won't help you produce a party in two months. This is why their voices mean nothing until they have a stake in the operation.

All of the above is especially true if you're working with two or more additional fraternities. The situation can become very convoluted, and making a clear distinction between those who have contributed financially and those who haven't makes it very clear who has a say.

Of course, you may need to have preliminary discussions to determine that you want to work with another fraternity, and that you share broadly similar visions of what you'd like to achieve. Beyond those preliminary discussions, however, you need to know that everyone who wants a voice in the creation of your event has skin in the game.

Establish a budget by the conclusion of your second conversation with your associates, sketch out your order of operations, and proceed accordingly. After that, they have a voice only when they bring money to the table. Do not wait on them to the point where you begin to harm your own capacity.

This is not about being a jerk. The first thing any band or agent will ask for when you confirm a booking is a deposit. Failing to provide them with a timely deposit can negate your agreement.

Producing a formal offer takes a lot of work, and you may be waiting on a response for a few weeks. If the agent or band agrees to your offer, they will send you a contract to sign, and they'll require you to return it with a 50 percent deposit. If you're not ready to give them a deposit, someone else may book them for your intended date.

Even if you know you will have the money in two weeks, you're asking for trouble. For this reason, you expect everyone involved in the process to make financial contributions promptly, as a sign of good faith. It's not because you're a stickler; it's because you will need their money to confirm acts.

THE ADVANCE

A few days prior to the show, you need to have an in-depth discussion with everyone who is working the show. That includes your sound engineer, your lighting designer, the company you're renting the stage from, and whoever is providing your generator. Reach out to them, and make sure that they have all the information they need. If they don't, make sure that you provide it for them.

In chapter 8 of this book, we'll discuss the concept of a formal advance. That is a crucial part of your preparation. For now, however, we're talking about having a checklist, making sure that you know what needs to be done, and talking to the people you will be relying on during the show.

Think about the amenities you will be providing. When the band pulls up, where will you put them? Do you have a green room? Have you even considered what constitutes a green room?

Another aspect of event production that is often overlooked is stage security. People assume that, because they're paying an off-duty police officer $25 an hour to sit in a chair and talk to girls, their security is covered. It really isn't.

You'll also need to make sure that someone is in charge of setting up and getting your acts on stage on time. Unless it's something you want to do, you need to delegate to one of your fraternity brothers (someone you trust to stay sober and be responsible) or hire a stage manager.

When bands show up, they will have a lot of questions. Some of those will be directed toward the sound engineer, and possibly to the lighting designer, but remember that it's not the sound engineer's job to walk the band on stage, show them their marks, and help them to load and unload their gear.

An exception to this is if you negotiate in advance with the sound engineer, in which case he will probably bring someone else on board to do that job.

The role of the stage manager is *not* interchangeable with the role of stage security. The stage manager's job is to work with the artists to make sure they have what they need and that they're on stage at the right time, in the right place. The job of stage security is to keep people off the stage and keep everything, and everyone, on the stage safe.

If you try to cut corners, and your stage manager is busy doubling as a security guard, he won't be any use to the band. Band members don't want to be removing the opener's drum kit, and they won't be pleased if you leave them without the crew they need.

Your back-of-house security is a further distinct role, similar to stage security but focused on anything that isn't on stage. If you decide to turn your spring party into a day festival, you will have thousands of people wandering around, becoming progressively more intoxicated as the event proceeds.

Think carefully about the timing of your show and who you will need to be present at what times. The people setting up the barricades need to be there well before the show starts. You don't want them to be installing barricades while people are showing up.

It's your job to ensure that people are there when they need to be. You will be the person who takes the flak if something goes wrong, and there's only one of you. If you're off fulfilling a hospitality rider or seeking out organic cigarettes because the band says they won't go on stage without them, you can't be watching over the stage or making sure the green room is secure. Unless you want the event to degenerate into chaos, you need to delegate.

Of course, as much as possible you need to be on hand to deal with any problems as they arise, so it makes more sense to delegate any last-minute hospitality requests to one of your fraternity brothers while you hold steady at HQ.

IN SUMMARY

The principles in this chapter can be applied to any party you're planning, at any time of year. Use them well, and they will serve you. In case you ever feel lost and uncertain of your next move, know that they are available for you to refer to again and again.

In the next part of this book we'll talk about what you need to do to produce your events, from contacting agents and making formal offers to booking sound engineers and lighting designers, and including all the things that most social chairs completely ignore, to their detriment and the detriment of their party.

PART TWO

—

EXECUTION

"A chain is no stronger than its weakest link."

WILLIAM JAMES

"I love it when a plan comes together."

JOHN "HANNIBAL" SMITH, THE A-TEAM

NOW YOU'RE THE PRODUCER

—

You've established your budget. You know your dates. Now, how do you actually go about booking a band?

You've never done this before, and you don't really know what you're doing. This section of the book will explain to you in detail exactly what protocol you need to follow and whom to contact. By the time you've read it, you'll know how to secure a booking with a band, how to book your production, and how to execute your events.

You'll learn about key parts of the process, such as submitting a formal offer and how to handle waiting on a response. You'll understand what you need to do once an artist confirms your formal offer.

When planning your production, it's important that you

establish good lines of communication with your sound engineer and your lighting director. They need to understand the needs of the bands you're booking and the number of people you expect to be at the party. They can help you interpret tech riders and let you know which parts are important and which are redundant.

You need to understand the details of the booking process, and you need to make sure that you have adequate, but not excessive, production. You'll want to make sure that you have a solid handle on what you should do in the days and weeks leading up to your event, right up to the day of show.

You'll also learn how to procure a hold on a venue. Unless you're holding your parties at your fraternity house, you'll need venues you can rely upon. Talent, production, and venue are the three legs of the stool when it comes to creating a successful event.

By the time you finish reading this section, you'll know everything you need to negotiate, organize, and run events like a pro. There are a lot of different ways to broker talent and book production. If you don't know what you're doing, there are also a lot of ways to get scammed.

That said, the challenges of putting together events properly aren't for everyone. You may decide that you don't want to go this deep into the difficulties of event management. In that case, you can skip to part three for information on how to sub out. There are some great services available if you want someone to take the load off your hands. It's never been easier to take a back seat and still run amazing parties.

BOOK YOUR ENTERTAINMENT

—

The first thing you need to know when booking a band is who represents them.

Unless you're looking at local acts, you can expect nine out of ten bands to have an agent or some other form of representative. The agent should be easy to find. Simply go to the band's Facebook page and look for the name and contact details of their representative.

Naturally, that person is working for the band, and the interests of the band are his main priority. The agent will try to convince you to pay as much money as he can. Be careful, and do not necessarily expect him to shoot you straight.

Once you understand this, you can decide which acts

you want to target. Different genres require different approaches.

A DJ, for example, is basically some guy playing music through his laptop. Before you pick up the phone and reach out to an agent, think about what will be involved in hiring a DJ. Maybe he will have a mixing board and some instrumentation that he will implement throughout his set, but unless you can provide him with good lighting, he will look less than impressive.

That means that, if he's playing outside, he will look a lot better in the dark. Booking a DJ for an outside daytime event is likely a lousy move unless you're willing to spend most of your budget making him look good.

Additionally, DJs need bass. Much of modern EDM (electronic dance music) is very bass-heavy. This gives you a unique conundrum. Bass cannot be pointed. It's omnidirectional, which means that if you have a neighbor who will complain about loud music late at night, you don't have many options for controlling low frequencies. Try to solve this problem by booking a DJ for a daytime slot, and you're back to the problem of his not looking good on stage.

To resolve these issues, your best fix is usually to take the DJ inside. A lot of people don't think about this and plan an outdoor party, which works fine until the headliner, who happens to be a DJ, walks on stage and wakes up the neighbors.

In summary, asking a DJ to headline an outdoor party at 10:00 p.m. is probably a bad idea. Consider bringing in a different act, or moving the party inside for the DJ set. Alternatively, book a more affordable regional DJ to play the late night set, using the expensive production you brought in for your headliner. In the event that the DJ gets shut down, you've only invested $1,000 or so in the talent.

These are things you need to be aware of before you pick up the phone to call an agent. As soon as you enter that conversation, the person on the other end of the phone will be trying to sell you on his talent. You need to know what you want before you let him do that.

As always, past performance is an accurate guide to future problems. Did your party get shut down last year because it was too loud? Did you turn down sound levels to accommodate the neighbors and wind up ruining the performance? Rap artists require many of the same low-end frequencies as DJs, but they usually play much shorter sets. If the DJ got shut down after an hour last year, could you risk bringing in a hip-hop act that will only play a forty-five-minute set?

Know your environment, and assess the potential based upon what has happened in the past and what you can expect to happen the night of your party.

Equally, know your chapter. You may have some great ideas, but you need to recognize what will appeal to your audience.

Maybe you have an uncle in the business, and he's telling you that a particular act will be huge in five years. That's great, but he may be too far ahead of the curve for the average partygoer. Five years down the road, they'll realize that they were incredibly fortunate to be at an early gig of a great band, but that won't win you friends or praise during your tenure as social chair.

It can pay to innovate and bring new talent to your chapter, but always remember that you were elected to represent them. Use your skill set to give them what they want.

Before you do any of the above, make sure that you're comfortable taking on the responsibility yourself. Ask yourself a simple question: Do I want to enjoy this event on the day of the show, or do I want to bask in the glory of having pulled off an insane party?

If you want to enjoy the event, you need to hire someone to do a lot of your work for you. It simply won't be possible to kick back and relax with your reputation, and your chapter's, on the line.

If you want to learn and grow from putting on the event, perhaps because you have ambitions of coordinating events in the future, go for it. Know, however, that you will be responsible for every moving part. You can't be drunk. You can't be watching the show with your girlfriend. You're going to have to be on call.

The decision is entirely yours, and it depends on your goals for the event. If you don't want to get into the nitty-gritty, sub out and bring in a production company or a turnkey event management company. If you decide to take the job on, do it well and with pride.

BOOKING A BAND

The first thing you need to keep in mind when booking a band is that everyone has an agenda, and it isn't the same as yours.

Whether you're dealing with an agent who is responsible specifically for the band you're interested in, someone within an agency that specializes in private events, or a company that offers middle buyer services, they will probably treat you as though you are guilty until proven innocent.

Unfortunately, a lot of fraternities have previously reneged on deals, failed to follow through on their promises, or thrown disastrous events. Even before you speak to an agent for the first time, he will be inclined to view you skeptically.

A lot of agents won't really want to work with you. They'll only want your money. This is not ideal, but it's a reality. Your professionalism can ease not only your own path but also the path of your fraternity brothers who will come after you.

Prepare effectively, know what you want, and ask smart questions. By the time you speak to an agent, you should know your dates and your budget, and he should be selling you on his talent. You don't want to waste time convincing him to do business with you because he doesn't believe you're for real.

All too often, people jump the gun and start talking to agents before they know what they want or how much they have to spend. Maybe they luck out and find an agent with good intentions, or maybe they don't.

Professionalism is the best antidote you have to the stereotypes associated with booking events in Greek life. Be as descriptive as you can about what you've got and what you need. If possible, provide schematics of your room and provide examples of bands that have played at your fraternity house previously; if you can name bands that are of comparable stature to the one you're looking to book, the agent will feel much more at ease about approaching them with your offer.

Many bands will take some convincing to play a fraternity house, so knowing that similar acts have already done so can take the pressure off.

Even party bands deserve your professionalism. They may not employ an agent, but they will still expect you to sign paperwork on time, provide them with a deposit, and organize a suitable green room.

The name of the agent listed at the band's Facebook page may not be the person you get through to. Larger agencies will probably put you through to an assistant, or even the head of the private events department.

Someone whose job is to book talent specifically for private events will be much more in tune with your needs, because the primary focus of her job is to handle events like yours. On the flipside, she will want to sell you what she has, not necessarily what you want.

Whenever you're dealing with an agency that has an exclusive roster, they have a vested interest in selling you acts that they represent. Using a turnkey company can take away this headache, because they don't care who they're booking. They're interested in giving you what you want.

When you start talking to an agent, expect a game of cat and mouse. Agents will want to know your budget, and you won't want to tell them. Unless you're working with a turnkey operation that represents you, and you alone, it's not a good idea to tell them your entire budget.

If your total budget is $20,000, that money needs to cover entertainment, production, hospitality, and tech riders. There's no sense showing your cards and letting an agent know how much you have to spend.

Some will be honest with you and let you know that you will need to direct some of your budget to backline and other expenses. They understand that you're new to your role, and they want the event to be a win for everyone involved.

Others will simply try to get as much money as they can out of you. If you tell them that you have $20,000, you will find that their act magically costs $20,000. This is why you need to do your research, find out how much you actually have to spend on entertainment, then lowball it slightly to give yourself some breathing space.

You're not trying to be deceitful, but you recognize that there's a high probability that unexpected expenses will arise. Maybe you need to provide in-ear monitors at the last minute, or the band decides to fly in to the show rather than drive, and they need backline.

Always leave a small proportion of your budget on the table to cover situations like this. You can rest assured that, if something happens, the band and the agency won't offer you a reduction because you didn't budget properly.

If you have a $20,000 budget, and you know that your production costs will be $4,000, say that you have $13,000 to $16,000, and let the agent present you with some options. Ask to see some possibilities at the bottom end of the range, as well as the top, to make sure that they're not inflating prices based on getting as much out of you as possible.

I was an agent for years, and a good agent won't want to take all your money if it means that his client will have a terrible experience. Don't misunderstand: *Every* agent wants all your money, and they may try to convince you to spend more than you need. Watch for tricks such as sending over a tech rider that would be more suitable for Madonna than a fraternity party. The sensible ones, however, realize that sending their bands into a nightmare scenario will result in earache when they have to hear all about it.

Nonetheless, there are some snakes out there who care *only* about maximizing their returns, even at the expense of their talent. Keep your eyes open, and be prepared to back off if you get a vibe you don't trust.

Mess this phase up, and you can find yourself having signed a contract and paid a deposit, and suddenly looking at an extra $5,000 in expenses you hadn't bargained for. The agent won't help you, because he has a contract saying it's your problem.

When you find yourself scrambling for additional budget, you might be tempted to transfer the shortfall on to your production guy. The result will be an unhappy production guy, sound quality that doesn't do a good job of conveying the awesomeness of the band, and a show that leaves a bad taste in everyone's mouth. Production isn't sexy, but things get very unsexy, very fast, when you don't allocate enough of your budget to it.

Up to a certain point, production costs are static. If you have a $10,000 budget, you may need to devote $5,000 to production. That probably seems ridiculous to you. It's not ridiculous, because if you had a $15,000 budget, you would still only need to spend $5,000 on production.

A stage, lights, sound, and a generator cost money. With a few subtle changes, that setup will accommodate a $20,000 band as well as it will accommodate a $5,000 band. By the same token, it will serve two thousand people as well as it will serve one thousand people.

Most of the time, if you get a tech rider with outlandish costs, a good production guy can bring them down for you. This is why it's so important to show your tech rider to your sound engineer and your lighting designer and ask them to provide a quote for you early in the process.

A good production guy is worth his weight in gold, so take the time to find one. Talk to people who have worked with whomever you're interested in hiring. There are a lot of good young sound engineers, who will be very good one day, but who are not necessarily the people you want working on an event with a national act in a tumultuous environment.

Ask yourself what they will do if the power goes out or a barricade gets knocked over. It's worth paying for experience and knowing that you have the situation in hand. It's a great feeling to know that you trust your production guy, who understands your requirements, and that you can go into conversations with agents well informed and certain you won't let yourself be ripped off.

Your sound engineer will take your audio rider and let you know what you need in terms of monitors and subs and speakers and mixers. He will set up your stage and make sure that everything is properly miked. He should work with the tour manager during the advance to ensure that everything is ready to go.

Similarly, your lighting designer handles the lights and should communicate directly with the band after you facilitate an introduction. Keep in mind that, unless you outsource the process to a turnkey company, you will need to perform the introduction and check that the process is moving smoothly.

Your job extends to managing your lighting designer and your sound engineer, but not to the technical aspects of their jobs. They need to check in with one another, because they will both need to move gear onto the stage within a relatively limited time frame. If they try to do this at the same time, they will get in one another's way.

You must make sure that they know when to load in and set up, and then trust them to do what they do best. These people are specialists in sound and lighting. They're not necessarily good business people, and they're not necessarily good with other people. It's your job as producer of the event to give them what they need to do a good job.

THE FORMAL OFFER

When you've got your tech rider, and you know exactly how much you have to spend on your entertainment, it's time to put in a formal offer.

A formal offer is a legally binding written document stating your interest in securing a band's services and the terms of the offer. Once you have submitted a formal offer, it is out of your hands. You must wait for the band to accept or reject it.

To create a formal offer, you need to make it clear when and where you want the band to perform and how much you're willing to pay. It should also detail who pays for additional expenses such as hospitality and production costs.

Your formal offer will be relatively simple, because you're running a private party. You'll be dealing in what's called a flat guarantee; a specific fee for services rendered. When artists perform in venues selling tickets, they sometimes expect a commission on ticket sales. That's not something you need to concern yourself with, so your formal offer can be very straightforward.

Most reputable agencies will be able to provide you with a template if you need one. If they do this, make sure you read the fine print and understand what you're signing.

A lot of offer templates say that all hospitality requests will be met, or that a tech rider will be provided to the artist's specification. This can be a pretty sketchy situation for you, because it puts you on the hook for whatever the artist desires. Don't sign anything legally binding before making sure that you're not opening yourself up to be liable for unlimited expenses.

A lot of agents ask you, casually, to submit a formal offer. Realize that, when they do this, they are inviting you to enter into a contract that will be legally binding if they accept your offer.

Don't submit more than one formal offer at a time unless you want to confirm more than one band. It's an excellent idea to impose an expiration date on your formal offers, so that agents and bands can't sit on them indefinitely.

They may be dealing with several formal offers at one time. Meanwhile, you have a party to plan. If you make it clear that your offer expires in five or ten business days, you won't find yourself in the awkward position of waiting six weeks for them to respond, all the while being unable to submit another formal offer. You'll know that, after giving them a reasonable period of time, your offer will expire and you can go elsewhere. This is where a lot of young people make mistakes, because they don't understand the legal ramifications of submitting a formal offer and how to protect themselves from being screwed.

A formal offer is an acknowledgment of exactly what you're asking of an entertainer and what you're offering them. An agent, in turn, will take the offer and draft an offer sheet that he will submit to the artist's management.

They will go over the offer, in conjunction with the band, and respond through their agent. If they want more money, or any other part of the offer to be altered, you'll hear about it from the agent. At this point, you have the opportunity to accept their terms or to stick with your original offer.

When you submit a formal offer, it's very important that you provide correct and precise information. Some of this is obvious, some less so. Your formal offer should include the following:

1. The date of your event

2. The name and address of the venue

3. The artist's name

4. The load-in time

5. The time you want your artist's set to begin

6. The proposed duration of the set

7. Any curfews that are in effect

Including the proposed set duration is very valuable for a number of reasons. First of all, pinpointing how long your artist will play for reduces the chances that they'll show up, play for half an hour, and leave.

It's also useful because you may be organizing a four-hour event, but you probably won't be expecting a single band to play for four hours. You need them to know when they're expected to arrive, what time they will be on stage, and for how long.

If you're not yet certain of the exact timing, write "per advance." For example, you might write: "Proposed set time is 9:00 p.m. to 10:30 p.m., per advance." You'll iron this out in the advance, which takes place five to ten days prior to the show, and it gives you some flexibility in case plans change.

Calculate the load-in time by thinking about how long the band will need to get set up. Do you want them to start their set at 10:30 p.m.? You may need them to load in at 8:30 p.m. Again, use the phrase "per advance." This indicates that the load-in time will be confirmed during the advance.

Be *very* specific when quoting dates and times. If your party will be taking place on September 9, include the year and the day of the week. If the date and the day don't match, your offer will be invalid or, if you're lucky, the agent will come back to you and ask for clarification.

On the other hand, if you make a mistake with the date and *don't* include a day of the week, you may sign a legally binding contract for the wrong day.

When you give them a load-in time and a time for the set to commence, specify whether it's a.m. or p.m. These small details may seem unnecessary, but you're communicating with people who receive a lot of information. You don't want to create any excuse for miscalculations.

Further down the offer, you'll need to describe the terms of the offer in detail. Lay out what you're prepared to pay them, and be sure to spell it out in words as well as numbers. It should look something like this: "$10,000 (ten thousand dollars)."

Your formal offer is a legally binding document. If you make a typo because you're tired or distracted, and add an extra zero, you are liable for the consequences.

If you offer a flat guarantee, this means that you agree to pay the stated sum and nothing else. In this case, make it clear that additional items, such as flights, ground transportation, and accommodation, will not be provided.

Alternatively, if you prefer to cover some or all of these expenses, factor them in when making your offer and hold back the necessary funds. There's no wrong way to do this. You can include or exclude whatever you want. It's very important, however, that you are specific.

If something goes wrong, and there are gray areas that haven't been covered, there's no chance that the band's agent and management will be knocking on your door to admit fault. Quite the opposite—they'll be trying to make out that any fault is yours. Don't give them ammunition.

Your formal offer will also need to provide buyer information and give the name of the signatory. You'll probably want to list your chapter as the buying company, and you will be the signatory, which means that you are the person signing the contract and taking responsibility for making sure that it's correct.

The offer needs to include your contact information. It also needs to include the contact information of your production manager. You may have hired a production company or a turnkey service to run the event for you, in which case give their details.

Otherwise, you're the point man, and you need to list production details for the sound engineer, the lighting designer, and the stage manager. Unless you have a solid understanding of stage plots, input lists, and backline requirement, you will not be much help in this area. Your job is to connect the band, and their management, with the guys who speak the language of production.

The band's agent or management will compile everything you give them into an offer sheet and present it to the band. If they confirm the offer, it will go straight into the contract, and correcting any mistakes will become a painful process. This is why it's a good idea to get the details right the first time.

It's also a very good idea to include an expiration date on your offers. Without one, you can technically be held to them months later. If you're booking a party two months out, you don't want to be waiting three weeks for a band to respond to your offer, putting you under the gun if they reject it. Write something to the effect of: "This offer expires in five business days."

If you're booking a national act for an event that's six months out, you need to adjust your expectations accordingly. They will probably take at least a few weeks to get back to you, and you need to set a realistic expiration date. If you make an offer to a $40,000 national act, and tell them it expires in three business days, they won't give you the time of day. If you're booking a party band for an event in a couple of months, and you give them twenty-eight days, you could be left hanging with no chance of booking another band.

Another useful phrase to insert into the offer is "mutually agreeable hospitality and backline provided by the purchaser."

"Mutually agreeable" is a very useful phrase. It means exactly what it appears to mean. You are not tied to providing anything that you don't agree to.

The band can come back to you and expect two hundred organic cigarettes and a dozen bottles of specialty tequila, and tell you that they won't accept your offer unless you agree to those demands. It's more likely, however, that you'll receive a formal contract, and your specification of mutually agreeable hospitality gives you the power to go through and strike out any requests that you deem unreasonable.

Remember that you are paying the band a lot of money to play a private show. It's not necessary for them to expect an expensive hospitality rider in addition to their fee.

If you get the contract back, and it states that the band wants $100 worth of fine cigars and a bucket of red M&Ms, you can reference the formal offer and say that you don't consider that mutually agreeable, and make a counter offer such as water, a case of beer, and pizza.

You're always free to do that; it's your money. Putting the term "mutually agreeable" in the formal offer, however, places you in a stronger position if you need to negotiate.

Of course, this works both ways. "Mutually agreeable" hospitality means that the band, or their manager, must agree that what you are offering to provide is acceptable. Don't try to stiff them. It will only create bad blood.

There are a lot of aspects of a typical formal offer that you don't need to worry about, because you're organizing a private event, not a ticketed event. Ticket sales and the date tickets go on sale are irrelevant to you.

Understanding what needs to go into a formal offer, and what doesn't, will equip you to make sense of an agent's template and adjust it as necessary. You can use the template they send you, but be aware that it will be weighted in their favor. Knowing your way around a formal offer redresses the balance.

THE CONTRACT

Congratulations. You've submitted a formal offer, it has been accepted, and the agent's assistant has issued you a contract. Now, all you need to do is sign it and return it with a deposit, and your show is confirmed.

Hold up a moment. Before you sign, be very sure that the contract in your hands matches the offer you presented.

First and foremost, check the hospitality rider, tech rider, and transportation terms. Go through with a fine-tooth comb and check the terms. In all likelihood, the agent's assistant hasn't given the contract a lot of thought, so there may be some conditions in there that don't meet your stipulations.

For example, the contract may contain a clause that reads: "Purchaser agrees to provide and pay for sound and lighting to meet with artist's specification and approval. Failure to present the engagement shall not relieve the purchaser of the obligation to pay the guarantee in full."

That's standard operating verbiage for a contract. The

only problem is that you didn't offer to supply sound and lighting that meet the artist's specification and approval. You offered mutually agreeable production, hospitality, and backline.

Making a change is as simple as striking through the phrase about sound and lighting being to the "artist's specification" and replacing it with the term "mutually agreeable specification." For this show to work, both parties must agree to the terms of the contract, so all you're doing is asserting your right to a say in the specifications of the lighting and the sound.

The point is, of course, that you need to know what you're looking for. If you neglect to alter the contract, you can find yourself on the hook for whatever sound and lighting the artist deems necessary, or they're within their rights to walk away and keep the deposit you gave them.

Be very honest about what the hospitality rider will provide. Don't allow yourself to be taken advantage of; the band doesn't need $700 worth of liquor. On the other hand, understand that they live on the road and that you need to keep them happy so that they perform well. Give them water, drinks, and finger foods so that they have a good experience.

You have the right to go through the hospitality rider and strike through any requests you consider unreasonable. They, in turn, have the right to come back to you and tell you that your offer is not meeting their needs.

If that happens, your best bet is probably to offer them a buyout. A buyout is an offer of cash in lieu of services. Instead of agreeing to provide $700 worth of high-end tequila, you might offer $300 in cash. You don't need to send someone to the liquor store, and they can do whatever they want with the money. It's a good way to find common ground and get to what's mutually agreeable.

Keep in mind that it's your job to catch things like this when you receive the contract. If you fail to, you can't complain when the band arrives and they expect you to supply them with whatever they want.

The same goes for the tech rider. If you initially took the tech rider the agent provided you with to your production manager or your sound engineer, and they struck through some aspects of it, make sure that those aspects haven't crept back into the contract. You may need to strike through them again to drive home the point that you are not willing to meet those specifications.

Approach flights, ground transportation, and lodging in

exactly the same way. Your band's agent and management may try their luck and slide clauses into the contract requiring you to cover the cost of any or all of these things. The next thing you know, you've put your signature to a document promising that you will put your DJ up in a five-star hotel.

It is 100 percent your responsibility to catch things like this. Don't ever sign a contract without making sure that you know *exactly* what you're agreeing to.

Most contracts come with a cover sheet, which details the basic terms of the agreement, and several pages of standard terms and conditions. Unless you're pre-law, and you get a kick out of examining the terms of contracts, your best bet here is to turn the contract over to your lawyer. Depending upon the quality of your relationship, this should cost you anywhere from $50 to $400. It will be money well spent.

For example, there may be a clause in the contract that states that no photography or reproduction is permitted and that attendees are not permitted to record, broadcast, or photograph the artists.

You know as well as the agent that smartphones exist, and it's not realistic to ban them from the performance, so you can strike through the clause and state that people can't be prevented from using smartphones.

The agent may look at it and demand that you *do* prevent people from using smartphones, but it's more likely that they will understand where you're coming from.

The main body of the contract will go into detail about the exact terms of artist compensation, and other important but boring subjects such as how to give notice to the artist's representatives if anything changes. You may see a clause relating to ticket sales, which is obviously irrelevant because you're putting together a private event.

The moral of the story is that you shouldn't simply sign and return the contract you receive, assuming that it conforms exactly to your formal offer. It may not.

If you want to learn how to peruse the contract yourself, get a lawyer involved the first time you're signing one, and keep a record of her work so that you'll have it to refer to the next time you're in a similar position.

It's worth noting that the advice above assumes that you are dealing with a reputable agency that understands the rules and acknowledges your right to contest parts of the contract. Should you find yourself entering into a contract with a fly-by-night agency, or the cousin of a rapper who fancies himself an agent, these rules may not apply.

Do not try to handle these scenarios alone or rely on unqualified help. Your fraternity brother's dad, who specializes in divorce law, may not understand the nuances of entertainment contracts and wind up making matters worse. Any situation that veers toward the shady calls for the expert help of an experienced middle buyer or turnkey company.

Finally, make sure that you get a fully executed contract.

At the bottom of the cover page, you'll see space for two signatures. One is for the name of your fraternity house and your signature. The other is for the artist or their management. The agent won't be mentioned.

Only when the artist or their representative signs the contract can you consider it fully executed. When you've signed it, it's a buyer-signed contract. At that point, you must request that it is signed by the artist or their representative and returned to you, otherwise it's highly unlikely that you'll ever receive a fully executed contract.

The reason for this is that, if neither the artist nor their representative signs the contract, they can claim that they have never seen your alterations. This gives them plausible deniability or, in plain English, the right to be a pain in your ass.

If they show up and demand their cigars and five-gallon bucket of red M&Ms, it's much more effective to present them with a fully executed contract than a buyer-signed contract. The former says that they have agreed to the hospitality you offered them. The latter only says that you struck through their requests.

The agent and the artist's management will not actively seek to make your life easier. They won't suggest that you go through the contract and strike out anything you don't agree to. They won't suggest that they sign the contract and return it to you fully executed. They want to keep the upper hand. It's your job to make sure that you cover your bases.

ARTISTS AND AGENTS

The vast majority of bookings take place through an agency, and it's in your best interests to use an agent. Reputable artists adhere to protocol. Those that are big enough to warrant engaging an agent should do so.

If that's not the case, you should ask yourself why. The probable answer is that they want to avoid paying commission, so they're boxing out their agent. You might get a lower price, but you're cutting out the guy whose job it is to make sure that the transaction runs smoothly.

Agents often get a bad rap, and almost as often they deserve it. Nonetheless, remember that trying to negotiate a deal without them hugely increases the potential for snafus and foul-ups. Agents are there to make sure the deal is conducted efficiently. They won't, however, prevent you from getting screwed. That's your job, or your middle buyer's.

Artists are often difficult to work with, because they're not business people but artists. If you deal directly with them, you're taking away the safety net of going through an agent, and you're dealing directly with an artist who you already know is trying to cut their agent out of the deal. Those should be red flags.

Additionally, dealing directly with an artist only gains you access to them, not to the entire roster of an agency. It won't help you set up future business opportunities, unless you want to book the same band several times.

An agency offers you protection if anything goes wrong. This is especially true in the EDM world and the hip-hop world, where artists are notoriously volatile. If your entertainer doesn't show up, and you booked them through their cousin or their tour manager, you don't have any legal recourse. You're at the mercy of their own sense of honor.

Agencies such as CAA and William Morris Endeavor are ruthless, and they'll squeeze every dollar out of you, but ultimately they are reputable companies. They depend on their artists showing up, and they will maintain a level of accountability for their artists' behavior that you won't find outside a reputable agency.

Going through an agent will cost you more money, but it will be a much smoother experience. The EDM world, for example, is built on dance and rave culture. Historically, it has been a fairly grimy, drug-fueled scene. As the genre has risen to popularity, so has the culture it grew out of, breeding a unique variety of artist and a unique style of promotion.

A lot of the promoters are really little more than drug-addled fans of the music, who think that they can put on a good show. As a result, the artists themselves, along with their agents and representatives, have their guard very high.

They may seem like jerks, and they may *be* jerks, but remember that the world made them that way. EDM culture is inseparable from the music. If you're interested in booking jam bands, you will probably find yourself dealing with a bunch of bros who are out for a good time and who are pretty easygoing. EDM agents, on the other hand, may well ask for 100 percent of the fee up front and screw you at any opportunity.

In fact, as the founder of a turnkey company that provides services to fraternities, I myself take a 100 percent up-front fee because I'm working with young people who can be volatile. That money is held in an account, and we can reassure artists that we have the funds. We pay them a 50 percent deposit on confirmation of the contract and the balance following their show.

I worked with a DJ once whose agency was demanding 100 percent of the fee up front. The company we booked through was reputable, but we had never worked with them before. I had to be very clear with them that I was not willing to part with 100 percent of the fee up front, because I would have no leverage. If the artist didn't show, I would be strung out.

In the end, I agreed to give them full payment directly prior to their performance. Even that was a risk, because they could have taken the money and dipped out after a twenty-minute set, but the agency was a large company, and I decided to trust them. I understood where they were coming from, because the genre can be extremely cutthroat. Fortunately, they understood my position, and we managed to cut a deal that worked for everyone.

They could have insisted on payment in full at the time of the booking. As they were a reputable company, I would probably have agreed. Nonetheless, it would have been a risk. When you're working with artists in the EDM genre, there's always a chance you'll encounter a fly-by-night sleazebag, whom you pay in full only for the artist to show up three hours late or not at all. When you hand over the entire fee before the performance, you relinquish your authority, and it's very difficult to get satisfaction if something goes wrong.

That's why there are companies specializing in client representation, talent buying, and event coordination. They sift through the dirt and make the process a lot simpler.

If you do find yourself in a situation where you need to defuse conflict, try and meet somewhere in the middle. Unless whomever you're working with is highly principled, or he's trying to screw you, you should be able to reach enough common ground to agree on a compromise.

You will reach a point where a line is drawn in the sand, and you'll need to decide whether the risk of something going wrong is large enough to make it worth letting the artist go. That's a good moment to call in a professional and ask for her counsel.

Hip-hop and rap artists, like EDM artists, have a reputation for being challenging to work with. Be prepared for that.

Jam bands, rock 'n' roll artists, and country musicians tend to be more laid-back, but they may bring more complicated technical requirements. Essentially, your average EDM act is a guy with a laptop who requires a couple of turntables and a mixer. He may desire a $50,000 lighting rig so that he looks cool, but his basic needs are very simple. At most, there will probably be two people on stage. It's a relatively simple environment to create.

Hip-hop is fairly similar. There's usually a DJ and at least one rapper, who uses a wireless microphone. Very often, a rapper's setup is almost identical to an EDM DJ's, except with one or more performers running around the stage with wireless microphones.

One hiccup to look out for, however, is that the gear used by DJs is constantly being updated. It's a racket. We're not talking about any great technological revolution here. Mixing boards are being produced with a few subtle changes, and of course the DJs all want the newest version.

The old ones become null and void for no real reason. Perhaps the USB portal is on the other side of the machine, or the new model has a built-in monitor. None of these changes are a problem until your DJ shows up expecting you to have the newest device, and you have a different version.

Not having a compatible backline can destroy a DJ or hip-hop set *very* quickly. Get the exact backline requirements in writing before the show, and make absolutely certain that you know what they need. Without it, maybe they can fake it by playing a Spotify mix or a SoundCloud mix, but otherwise your DJ may not be able to play at all.

Often, when you reach out to a rapper or his tour manager, he will say he needs one thing but needs something completely different. I have personal experience, many times, of artists telling me that they need a particular mixing board and then showing up without the right adapter to connect their laptop, their iPad, or their smartphone to the mixing board.

They have their backing music stored and ready to go in their audio device, but they can't connect it to the mixing board and therefore the speakers. For lack of an eighth-inch converter, the entire gig is on the rocks. This issue has literally been the downfall of innumerable hip-hop shows: an inability to connect the device where their backing music is stored with the hardware that propels sound.

Ridiculous as it sounds, this is your problem if they show up without the relevant adaptor. They will expect you to sort it out, and they may blow you off altogether if you can't fix it.

A great production manager or sound engineer will be worth their weight in gold here. These are the people who have hundreds of shows under their belts, and they know what to look out for.

The most likely groups to present a problem here are lower-tier hip-hop artists and what's euphemistically known as "heritage" hip-hop. "Heritage" is a more pleasant way of referring to guys who used to be big stars but who are now gigging purely to pay the bills.

In the heyday of their careers, these guys had people taking care of these things, so they're not likely to be savvy at doing it for themselves. They may box out qualified personnel so they can save money, and that makes it much more likely they'll turn up to play a show without some crucial piece of equipment.

Rock 'n' roll acts, party bands, and jam bands are a different story. They usually contain between three and ten members, all of whom need to be connected to monitors so they can hear themselves. They will have relatively complex backline requirements, and there will be a lot of moving parts to synchronize.

It's usually much easier to broker deals with bands of this type, and to work with them, but the technical execution can be a lot more complex.

For example, imagine that you've booked three bands onto your six-hour bill. You've gone through a solid agent, secured their services within your budget, and they've been totally cool with a mutually agreeable hospitality rider. So far, so good.

That is, until they arrive to play your show, and you realize that each one of the bands is expecting to play a two-hour set. You haven't built in any changeover time.

The absolute *minimum* time needed for a successful changeover is twenty minutes, and you should allocate half an hour to ensure a smooth transition. You need to account for the time it takes each band to strike their gear and get it off the stage, plus however long it takes the next act to come on, set up, and go through a line check.

To reduce the impact of this problem, consider asking bands to share backline. Each drummer will provide cymbals and a snare, while the rest of the kit remains set up throughout the show. This move alone can shave upwards of ten minutes off each changeover.

In this case, you need to make it very clear when you're submitting a formal offer and ratifying the contract that you will provide the backline, or that you are asking one of the bands to bring backline that will be used by all of them. You must also decide whether it makes more sense for the opening act to leave their gear on stage or for the headliner to set up early, assuming they're willing to let the opener use their kit.

Another way of handling this, if you have a large enough stage, is to set up the headliner's drum kit in the center of the stage, and the support act's kit in front or to the side, prior to the beginning of the show.

The chances are that bands will be familiar with these setups, and willing to work with you, especially if they have ever played in any densely populated city in the Northeast. No one enjoys lugging a drum kit up a narrow set of stairs so they can play a two-hundred-capacity club.

By the same token, any band that has played a festival probably understands the value of sharing backline for the sake of a smooth, swift transition.

If you have multiple entertainers on one bill, you may be able to mix and match. Bring a band in earlier in the day. They can play a longer set, and they make a more interesting spectacle during daylight hours than a DJ or hip-hop act.

When the sun goes down, that's the time for the rappers to come to the forefront. It's easy to make the changeover; the band need only strike gear, and rappers only need lighting and microphones.

If the party has a late-night portion, that's the perfect time to schedule a DJ set. Even more than hip-hop, DJs rely on lighting to make their performance effective. Plus, they can use almost exactly the same setup as rappers, except that they don't need as many microphones.

The easiest bands to accommodate are usually party bands. A large part of their appeal, aside from the fact that they play music everyone knows and spread a good vibe, is that they are usually self-contained. They provide a basic lighting package and a PA system, taking a load off your mind.

That said, most party bands won't provide a generator. If you have a band booked to play an outside show, you will need to make sure that they have access to quality power.

Quality power does not come from the generator you take on a camping trip to make sure that you can charge your cell phone. For LED lights, you will need something that offers clean current. There are plenty of companies that rent good-quality generators, and it will pay to forge a good relationship with one of them.

If the band is slated to play at your fraternity house, check that your power outlets can handle the band's power needs. To do this, ask the entertainer how many outlets they need and what wattage they require. Then, ask your adviser whether your house can meet those needs. If your adviser doesn't know, hire an electrician to test the outlets.

You may discover that a full-blown generator is overkill, and that hiring someone to tie in a distro to the power source will be sufficient.

However you do it, make sure you can provide for the band's power needs. I've lost count of the number of times I've seen a band come in, set up, and start rolling through their set. They look good, they sound good, and the room's rocking. What happens next? You guessed it: power outage.

Unless you're an electrician, the most sophisticated response you can probably conjure to this situation is to start flipping breakers, which probably won't work. Know your band's requirements before they arrive, and you will dramatically reduce the probability of this scenario becoming a reality.

Your other primary concern when you hire a party band is providing them with a suitable stage. Unless you book a very unique band that doubles as a production company, they will not bring a stage with them, so you need to make sure they have one.

Planning events becomes easier with experience, but you can reduce the stress by knowing what to expect. Think carefully about the likely needs of your artists and their probable blind spots, and prepare effectively.

Know that EDM acts and hip-hop artists may be difficult to work with, but their technical riders will be comparatively simple. Make sure that you have enough power to prevent an embarrassing outage in the middle of a set.

IT IS POSSIBLE

We've covered a lot of ground in this chapter, and it can seem daunting. If you take it step by step, however, you can negotiate with agents, book great bands, and experience the satisfaction of knowing that you've created an amazing show.

Alternatively, perhaps you're reading this and thinking that it sounds like far more work than you care to do. In that case, you can always sub out and find a reputable production company or turnkey operation to take much of the burden off your hands.

PRODUCE YOUR EVENTS

The first question you need to answer when producing an event is whether you want to do this yourself or outsource to a production company.

As discussed in the introduction to this book, if you choose to take on the production of your event, you will need to be sober, alert, and on call on the day of the show. You will not be able to enjoy the entertainment in the way that the average partygoer will.

If that's your preference, it can be very exhilarating to produce an event. If it's not, however, be honest with yourself and don't half-ass it. You will be letting yourself down, and more importantly you'll be letting down everyone who is relying on you to create a great show.

We've discussed some of the basics over the course of this book. For ease of reference, here they are again.

You will need a sound engineer. You will need a lighting designer. Unless you have an existing stage of sufficient quality to satisfy your entertainers, you will need a stage. You will require a power source, probably a generator or a distro from a reputable rental company. It pays to check in with the previous social chair and discover where they rented a generator.

Remember that all of the people listed above have an agenda, and their agendas will not match up perfectly with yours.

Your lighting designer will want to build the most extravagant lighting set possible. If you have a big-name DJ, that's probably what you want, because without it he'll look like a weirdo with a laptop. Otherwise, you'll want something smaller.

Your sound engineer will want to rent you the highest spec system available. If you're having a four-thousand-person event in your front yard, you'd better take his advice. If you have a couple of hundred mothers showing up to drink Bloody Marys with their sons before a football game kicks off, you don't need something nearly that fancy.

Your stage designer can set you up with something that looks like Bonnaroo, with a giant stage liner made of aluminum and lifted on hydraulics, but you probably don't need it. If I run a stage rental company and I own six stages, I want to sell you on the biggest one, even if it's totally unnecessary.

One area you should *never* scrimp on, however, is power. Power is at the core of all your operations. Nothing else that you do matters one iota if you don't have the power to make it happen.

Make sure that you have more than you need, because if you have an excitable lighting designer, those lights can suck down a whole lot of power. It's fine for the guy at the generator rental company to tell you their generator can handle a performance, but if your lighting designer is intent on illuminating the entire neighborhood, that won't help you. In short, be absolutely *certain* that you have enough power.

Know yourself. You are (hopefully) a responsible person. If you're reading this book, the chances are that you've taken the time to build out a checklist and to confer with people who have more experience than you.

You're still an amateur.

Be aware of that, and don't allow people to take advantage of you. At the same time, however, don't pretend that you know more than the professionals you're working with. Without them, you won't have a show, so you need to rely on them.

If someone put a gun to your head and insisted that you run the sound, or made the lights move, you wouldn't be able to save your own life. Keep that in mind, and you'll stay humble enough to do a good job. Once you've agreed to work with people, you need to trust them.

A common item that comes up in the technical rider is a drum riser, at a cost of between $200 and $400. Did the artist whom you booked specifically request a drum riser? If so, why? Is your stage large enough to comfortably situate a drum riser?

An expensive EDM duo, with one member playing the saxophone and the other playing the drums, probably *does* need a drum riser. Without it, the audience won't be able to see the drummer. A $2,000 jam band probably doesn't need a drum riser. It's unlikely the drummer will be visible no matter what you do, and it isn't a big deal.

This is something to discuss with the company you're renting your stage from. Hopefully, you have a good enough relationship with them that you can trust them to shoot you straight.

You can put yourself in a really difficult position in an attempt to save a little money. Perhaps you end up irritating your artist and they refuse to perform, or they perform but they don't look good, which is a waste of the thousands of dollars you spent on hiring them for the sake of a small saving.

The moral of the story here is that being an amateur puts you in a quandary. You don't have many past experiences to draw from, so it's difficult for you to know that you're making the right judgment call. You need to trust your suppliers, and yet you know they all have their own agendas. The best thing you can do is choose carefully whom you work with and trust them.

DON'T ANNOY THE BAND

Bands will walk if you don't take care of them properly, and you'd be foolish to think they won't.

As a rule, national acts do not see playing your fraternity house as an awesome experience. If they're from other countries, or other areas of the United States, they may have a very negative perception of Greek life.

In all probability, they want to show up, play, get paid, and leave. The last thing you want to do is fuel their negativity. Show them great hospitality, appreciate their work, and give them a positive experience. Not only will you increase the chances that they'll give you an incredible show, but you'll also do your successor, and every other chapter of your fraternity, a favor by making it easier to book the same act in the future.

They should want to play, because that's what they do for a living, but don't give them any excuse to bail on you. If you fail to honor part of the contract, that may be all they need to justify walking. Everyone wants a good experience, and your part of that is to treat the band well and make sure they have what they need.

Don't do things that make them feel your operation is sketchy, such as changing the venue on them at short notice. If something changes, let them know in good time, and make sure that they are aware of all relevant information.

There's nothing worse than taking a great band and pushing them into a tiny room with no stage, in an unsecured venue, and watching them grin and bear it to get through their set. If all you have is a small room without a stage, make sure they are made aware of that up front.

They may not want to play the gig, or they may find a way to make it work. Either option is better than having them arrive only to discover that the facilities are inadequate.

That's no way to promote goodwill.

Even when you're working with bands that provide lighting and sound, you still need to make sure that you're on top of the venue and communicating effectively with them about what they can expect. In the end, this is simply a matter of treating them with the respect with which you'd like them to treat you.

MANAGING YOUR PRODUCTION ENGINEERS

Sound engineers and lighting designers generally work differently than agents and managers. They may be happy with an agreement based on a handshake, as opposed to submitting a contract. Be a man of your word, and honor that agreement. These guys are not bloodthirsty sharks like the average agent, but that's no reason to ignore their needs.

Some, however, will send you a contract to sign. If they do, there's probably no need for you to mark it up, simply because you won't understand the industry jargon. You've given them a tech rider, and you need to trust that they will fulfill it. Unless you've spent the past few months studying sound engineering, this is no time to start micromanaging your sound engineer.

I've been guilty of this myself. Looking at a quote from a production company or a lighting designer, I've started to question the costs. Even as the words have left my mouth, however, I've realized that I need to shut up. If your production guys have been kind enough to itemize their quote, realize that you have no idea what the difference is between an XLR cable and an LED. The only thing to be gained from quizzing them is that you irritate them and harm your working relationship.

You can sit down in front of your computer for three hours and puzzle out the difference between different items of equipment, but that's a waste of your time. A production engineer who provides you with an itemized list of what you'll be getting is being very professional. Appreciate that, rather than questioning them excessively. If they're good, it will show in the performance.

In case you're still concerned about the integrity of your quote, nail down a price as far ahead of time as possible, and ask them to sign a document to the effect that the price won't increase between the date of the contract and the date of the show. That gives you all the ammunition you need to make sure that the price doesn't inflate, as long as your needs don't change.

A lot of young guys who want to be sound engineers will be willing to cut their prices to the bone in order to secure the gig. Cheaper is not necessarily better. Often, what you're paying for is not the quality of the gear; it's the experience of the old, salty guy with poor hearing who cusses a lot. He may seem ornery, but he will fix your problems when something goes wrong.

Having high-quality gear is great, but no gear is better than the guy operating it. Sometimes experience costs money, and if you've hired a $4,000 national act to come and perform in front of three thousand people in your front yard, money spent on knowing that your sound engineer knows what he's doing is money well spent.

Let your buddy who swears he's a sound engineer twiddle the dials when your other buddy's jam band is coming over to play a two-hour session on your back porch. When you have a major party to throw, you need to work with someone who has been thoroughly road-tested.

Protect yourself by asking prospective production engineers for references and examples of shows they've done. Just as you need to come correct when you're talking to agents who are wary about working in Greek life, you are totally within your rights to ask for proof of your production guy's track record.

The chances are that they'll list events that they worked at neighboring fraternity houses or your own, so you can go to previous social chairs and ask for their opinions. You may even find that you've attended some of their events yourself.

A lot of production companies are unwilling to work fraternity parties, because the money isn't great and there's a much higher likelihood of the gear being damaged than there is in more controlled settings.

In most markets, there are one or two companies that specialize in Greek life and who have gotten good at it as a result. Always look for a company that you've worked with in the past or that can give you solid references. Otherwise, there's a good chance that they are new to the business and don't understand what they're getting into.

OUTSIDE OR INSIDE?

Outside parties require more of everything: more power, more sound, more lights, a bigger stage, and more cover in case of rain. If you decide to have an outdoor party, you will spend more money. As a rule of thumb, if you have a $20,000 budget, it's realistic to expect that 25 percent of it will go toward production. If your budget is $10,000, as much as 50 percent of it may be spent on production.

From a cost standpoint, there are tremendous benefits to holding an event inside. You're working with a confined space where you have control of the elements. It's not going to rain on you. You can halve the number of lights you use and make twice the impact. On the other hand, if you want to create a festival atmosphere with bands playing throughout the day, and you've got a huge budget to play with, maybe it's worth it to you to go outside.

Think carefully about your choice of venue. A lot of your parties will take place at your fraternity house, but some won't. You need to match the venue with the event.

For a date night, a semiformal, or parents' weekend, do you need to seek out a more formal setting that's conducive to dancing and entertainment? On the flipside, if you want to have a really raucous party, are you looking for a place where you can damage everything in sight?

Your venue needs to match your party and your entertainment. Your buddy's jam band will be happy to play anywhere. A ten-piece party band that specializes in weddings and corporate events won't want to play in a dirty, smoky dive bar. This is the kind of band you'll be booking for parents' weekend and potentially paying $4,000 to $10,000 for, so give them a venue that suits both the band and the attendees. If they're playing at your fraternity house, give them a large enough stage and a proper green room.

Be aware of your limitations. If you're traveling, you may be in a hotel or a convention center. Check whether there's a curfew, and make sure you understand any regulations, especially sound regulations, associated with the venue and the town.

LIGHTING

There are three primary ways to make lighting effective. The first is simply to emit a ray of light that is visible from its source. The second is to illuminate the beam using haze or fog. The third is to bounce the light off other objects.

For outdoor events, you can make lighting more powerful by covering the stage and letting the lighting refract off the cover. You can also set up the stage so that lighting is shot up into the branches of trees. As long as it doesn't trigger the fire alarm, haze is especially effective indoors, where you can control the environment. Overall, you get far more bang for your lighting buck when you go indoors.

Whatever you do, make sure that you have enough power. Don't employ old lights that suck down a lot of power in an ancient fraternity house that has archaic wiring. That won't be good for business.

There have been numerous advances in lighting technology over the years, making it lighter, cheaper, and better than it has ever been before. By the same token, expectations are much higher than they used to be.

Bands that have been touring for many years now find that they need to travel with giant lighting rigs merely to stay competitive. This dynamic trickles down, affecting private events as well as ticketed ones. There are more lighting options than ever and more lighting designers excited to put them to work. You need to know the different kinds of lighting and what's suitable for your party.

Your primary concern should be power. Newer LED lights are very efficient and don't get as hot as older models, but some lights still use older technology. A good lighting designer should know the difference. If you have all the power you need for modern lighting, and then a lighting designer brings in older lights that have been superseded, suddenly you'll be struggling for power.

Different types of events require different standards of lighting. DJs, in particular, can look very silly without adequate lighting. More, however, is not always better. A skilled lighting designer can often do more with fewer lights, working in sequence, than an inexperienced designer with more.

Some lighting designers are one-trick ponies. All their designs look identical. This is fine for the genres they're best suited to, but it's limiting when applied to other genres. For example, maybe your lighting designer loves creating designs using LED bars or using an LED panel. This will look fantastic for an EDM or jamtronica act, but not for hip-hop or party bands.

Rap performances are best accentuated by strobes, which are actually cheaper than setting up an LED wall or a string of moving lights. Excessive lighting would detract from the focal point of the performance, which is the guy rapping into the microphone.

If you're booking a DJ, you may benefit from choosing a cheaper entertainer and a more expensive lighting design. With a rapper, the opposite is true.

Jam bands and Motown bands are entertaining in their own right, and their lighting needs differ again from DJs and rappers. Extravagant lighting designs may look good, but they clutter up the stage. Bands don't need a lot of additional lighting to look great. They need to be lit from below, in a way that illuminates their faces and bodies.

DJs, on the other hand, benefit from sick light shows that make them look imposing. Make sure that your lighting company understands your specific needs, and that they're not simply trying to take a one-size-fits-all approach to your lighting. Keep in mind that there's not always a direct relationship between the number of lights and the expense.

Sometimes you're paying for the qualified person who can execute your show.

AUDIO

If you pay $100 to see a reunited Guns N' Roses play at a fifty-thousand capacity stadium, you want to hear every note of that music exactly as it was intended.

For a fraternity party, good audio is important, but it's not as crucial as it is for a high-end ticketed gig. You're organizing a free party on a strict budget. At any given time, you can expect at least half of the attendees to be talking, socializing, hitting on girls, flirting with boys, or doing something else that isn't listening to the band.

You may have two thousand people coming to your party, but that doesn't mean you need a $4,000 line array rig. Realistically, probably only five hundred to one thousand of them will be listening at any one time, so you can use a rig that's suitable for one thousand people, and it will be plenty good enough.

A line array is an amazing technological achievement. By hanging speakers in an arc that projects sound out evenly across a large group of people, it makes huge shows in football stadiums possible. Cool though it is, however, you probably don't need it for your fraternity party. You need enough sound to achieve your goals, but you also don't want to spend a disproportionate amount of money on audio.

A good, high-quality rig will allow the people who choose to be close to the stage to listen, without blowing excessive funds on the audio. For most purposes, elevated speaker stacks will be totally sufficient.

For guidance, when you have fewer than two hundred guests you can use a DIY setup, which a small band will usually provide themselves. This consists of basic speakers elevated on sticks. Above two hundred attendees, you'll probably need something bigger than a personal PA system. This is the point at which you're looking to bring in a speaker stack, which will provide you with enough power for parties with a capacity of three hundred to six hundred people. Above around six hundred people, you will want to elevate your equipment, by setting it up on a stage on top of other gear or building wings onto the stage to give the speakers an additional few feet of height. When you're catering to more than one thousand people, double down on that, and you should be covered up to two thousand. Only then should you consider a line array.

Equally as important as the sound itself is the necessity of keeping people safe. Bass may be omnidirectional, but high-end frequencies such as guitar and vocals can be pointed in any direction. That means they can be pointed in people's faces and ears, potentially causing injury.

Speakers that are projecting high-end frequencies need to be situated at least six feet above ground level. If they are sitting on the ground, people can accidentally lean against them and rupture their eardrums.

It's not funny, and it's not cool. Irresponsibly sited speakers can cause hearing damage that will affect people for the rest of their lives. Know that if you use a hack sound engineer who doesn't know what he's doing, someone could go deaf as a result of his shoddy work. In addition, that person won't come after the sound engineer. He or she will come after you.

If you're having a small party in your fraternity house and you don't have a lot of lighting, you will probably be able to use your internal wall outlets to power your speaker system. In case that's not enough, a qualified sound engineer or an electrician will be able to tie a distro into your power source.

A distro creates a very powerful connection from your main power source, which can then be taken elsewhere through a giant cable known as a snake. This means you can forego using extension cords that run to great distances from your wall outlets, diminish power, create a trip hazard, and potentially overload your system.

There are stronger power cables you can use instead of extension cords, but a distro is usually the smarter option. Hiring someone to come to your fraternity house and tie in one of these devices runs to around $150, which is dramatically cheaper than using a generator, and a lot safer and more professional than relying on extension cables.

Nonetheless, if you *do* need a generator, get a generator. Perhaps you're having a party in your front yard and it's 250 feet from the nearest power source. Maybe your fraternity house was built in 1880, and it doesn't have adequate power to serve your party.

A high-quality generator should cost you $500 to $600, tops, and will provide enough power for all of your sound, lighting, and stage needs. Before you make a decision, ask your sound engineer and your lighting engineer to make sure the generator you're looking to hire is up to specification. To provide peace of mind that you have all the power you need, it's money well spent.

Many companies that rent generators impose an eight-hour usage limit and will charge you time and a half for operation beyond that limit. If you're running an all-day event, make sure that you shut off the generator when everyone leaves and the show's over, otherwise you can find yourself with a bill twice as large as you anticipated because the generator ran all night until it ran out of diesel fuel.

This is the kind of detail you won't need to concern yourself with if you have a production company running point on your events. If not, however, you can easily trip yourself up and cost your fraternity totally unnecessary money.

SECURITY

Imagine that you're a chef in a high-performance kitchen. You're trying to create amazing cuisine in a high pressure environment, and every three minutes a drunk girl bumps into you or a wasted bro vomits on your feet. It's not going to go well.

That's the position you're putting your artists and your sound engineer in if you don't provide them with proper security.

First and foremost, you need barricades to prevent people from jumping on the stage, interfering with your artists' performance, and potentially hurting themselves or damaging expensive equipment.

The random drunk girl who jumps on stage always gets

a good response from the crowd, but she doesn't know what she's stepping on or what she's interrupting. The entertainer may become so frustrated that he gives up and walks off stage.

The stage is also full of expensive gear, which can easily be damaged. If people get on stage, they can get hurt. It's fun to have a girl jump on stage and dance with the band, but it's also a grotesque risk. You need stage security to prevent it from happening or, if it must happen, to keep it orderly.

Girls travel in herds. They go to the bathroom together, and they will want to get on stage together. If one gets up there, another three or four will want to jump up as well. One person can comfortably handle three people, because they can gently grab one with their left hand and one with their right hand. The third will follow because she doesn't want to be up there alone. Any more than that, and one person won't be able to handle them with ease. Make sure that you hire enough people to conduct stage security. Also, consider installing some barricades to make their job easier.

Your artist isn't a security guard and doesn't want to be. He has no interest in looking like the bad guy by stopping his show and ushering someone off stage. This is the job of stage security, and it is essential. Security is there to make sure that your sound engineer, your stage manager, and your artist aren't called into action to evict drunk people from the stage.

Stage security needs to be well trained, polite, and assertive. They need to look the part. They are the primary barrier between drunk people who want to get on stage and the fulfillment of that desire. You don't want the performance to turn into a farce, however amusing that might seem for the audience.

In addition to stage security, you will need backstage security. Backstage is where things get broken, or stolen, or both. If you've got some guy lurking backstage with $10,000 of guitar cases and trussing, you're asking for trouble. Even if he doesn't have malicious intentions, he has probably been drinking. The next thing you know, he's urinating on your power source or he's got his hands in the guacamole. This is why you need backstage security.

You may have some problems with people complaining that this is their fraternity, and their money paid for the party. That's true, but the backstage security guy is ensuring that their money is spent on a great party, rather than reimbursing an angry artist for damage to their equipment. Good security is your friend, not your enemy.

Your first line of defense, before partygoers even reach the security guys, should be a set of barricades. It's important that you have some form of barrier between the general population and the stage/backstage area.

For a small party, the barrier may be primarily psychological. A series of wooden stakes hammered into the ground and connected by a brightly colored ribbon may be enough. Obviously, that won't hold people back if they are committed to getting past it, but the simple fact of acknowledging a barrier makes the job of the security guards easier.

The next step up from a ribbon could be construction fencing. Again, this can be crossed very easily, but it forms a first line of defense. Beyond construction fencing, you can employ a form of barricade known as bicycle racks, named because they resemble bicycle racks.

These are very effective. Their only weakness is that eventually they can be pushed forward, meaning that a straight line of bicycle racks can be made to cave inward in the middle.

For a very large act, you may want to invest in proper barricades, which are known as blow-through barricades. These are employed at festivals and political rallies. No amount of pressure from the crowd will knock them down.

They are expensive. You may spend $800 securing your stage. On the other hand, they provide extremely good protection, and they also include pedestals from which security guards can observe the entire crowd. This allows them both to make sure people aren't breaching the perimeter and also to look out for anyone who is dehydrated, who has had too much to drink and is passing out, or who is being assaulted.

Another advantage of blow-through barricades is that they protect the stage. Some stages are extremely strong, but most are not built to withstand pressure from the front. A thousand people pushing a stage from the front can topple it, leading to serious injuries or even killing people. For very high-energy acts, such as certain rappers and DJs, investing in proper barricades is a requirement.

THE GREEN ROOM

Where should you situate your green room?

The obvious choice is probably to use somebody's room. The problem you will run into, however, is that people feel a justifiable sense of entitlement when their dues are being used to hire a band and they find that the band has taken over their room. It can be very difficult to explain to those people that the green room is off-limits.

You will always encounter some dickhead who wants to go into the green room and get the rapper high or do drugs with the band. Not only is this clearly illegal, it can result in the cops raiding you and getting your show shut down.

I've seen this happen. Some guy who wanted to be cool started smoking weed with the rapper, prior to the show. When the rapper's tour manager cracked a window to let the smoke out, three cops, who knew there was a party brewing and were looking for an excuse to pounce, arrested the rapper and the guy who was supplying him. The show got shut down, and the fraternity was out $20,000, for no return.

If someone wants to be a hero and smoke with the rapper, insist that he waits until after the show. At least, this way, if he gets busted, it won't ruin the night for everyone else.

Often, the idea of a proper green room is dismissed as a minor concern. It shouldn't be. It's very likely that you'll be keeping $10,000 worth of equipment in there, so you need to know that the room is lockable. You also need it to be close enough to the stage for the artist to get from the green room to the stage without being bothered, and for their gear to be transported quickly and easily.

Your artists need to be 100 percent comfortable that the

green room is secure. They want to prepare for a show in peace and quiet. They have a lot of expensive equipment that they do not want to see damaged or stolen. They may have a wad of cash that you've given them for the show. Obviously, you do not want to open yourself up to accusations that the cash has taken a walk on your watch. Unless you can guarantee the security of the artist, their gear, and their hospitality rider, you don't have a formal green room.

Some bands are amazing performers but total sleazebags on a personal level. If the room is insecure and girls get into the green room, videos of them using drugs could find their way on to YouTube. Worse yet, someone could register an accusation of assault, costing you thousands of dollars in lawyer's fees and a colossal headache. The only way to be totally safe is to maintain a complete separation between the artists and the general population. That means the green room needs to be monitored constantly, which is very difficult to do if it's in your fraternity house and the party is in the front yard.

A much more sensible solution would be to rent a twenty-foot-by-twenty-foot tension tent, and shell out an extra $200 to have a couple of walls set up so that people can't see inside it. If you locate it behind or beside the stage, it can double as a staging facility and a place where artists can relax out of the sun or the rain.

You may not want to spend $500 to $700 on erecting a tent to use as a green room, but that money could save you a lot of trouble. Maybe you can save on the cost of production personnel because it acts as a staging ground and you don't need to employ as many production personnel. Maybe it prevents you from getting sued by the artist because his $3,000 Les Paul guitar doesn't get damaged.

A good green room is an important part of your show, and sometimes it's worth spending a little extra money to make sure that artists are secure and in close proximity to the stage.

STAGE MANAGEMENT

Stage management is often overlooked because inexperienced social chairs assume that the production manager is also the stage manager. This is not the case.

The stage manager's job is to make sure that the band is on stage when they're supposed to be on stage and to check that they have microphones, stage directions, and beverages.

Stage managers are responsible for walking the band up to the stage with a flashlight so they can see where they're going in the dark. They're responsible for giving the band a five-minute warning so they come off stage in time. Stage managers usually help with tasks such as disassembling the band's drum kit so that they can get off stage in a timely fashion.

They are especially useful when there is more than one entertainer on the bill, because those are the occasions when you will be running on a tight schedule and you need someone to keep track of time. If you don't hire a stage manager, you will soon discover that you are the stage manager, and if you aren't up for the job, you will invite chaos.

YOUR RESPONSIBILITIES AS THE EVENT ORGANIZER

As social chair, you are responsible for hiring people to fill all of these positions unless you delegate that role to someone else. If you've hired a lighting director, a sound engineer, and a security manager, but you forgot to hire a stage manager, you get to be a stage manager for the evening.

If you did all of the above and also forgot to hire someone to work the door on the green room, suddenly you're doing two jobs at once. If you *also* neglected to equip the green room properly, you're doing both those jobs *and* you'll need to go off site to get food and beer and cigarettes for the band. It's physically impossible. You cannot be in three places at once. This is why you need proper support.

When you choose to produce an event yourself, there's a

proper way to go about it. You can do this, but you'll need to be organized, create a checklist, and hire the people you need to help you, because anything that you don't delegate effectively becomes your problem.

THE ADVANCE

—

Performing an advance is the single most important thing you can do to make sure that your event runs successfully. A good advance will make your party, and not advancing your show can break it.

What exactly *is* an advance? It's an action taken by the production manager anywhere between five and ten days prior to the day of a show. The production manager approaches each vendor, each tour manager, and anyone else with responsibility for an element of the performance and confirms everything that has been previously established.

You may wonder why it's necessary to go over agreements that have already been made. The simple answer is that things change. If you booked an artist two to six months out, even a slight alteration could have a profound effect.

For example, perhaps you learned recently that the curfew at your fraternity house is 11:00 p.m. instead of midnight. Have you conveyed that to everyone involved in the show, or will they be arriving thinking that the curfew is midnight?

Maybe you've been planning an outside event, but the weather forecast a week out tells you that there's a hurricane coming in, rendering an outdoor event senseless. Have you communicated that to everyone with a stake in the party?

You probably brokered the show with the artist's agent. That's fine, but when the artist arrives, the agent will be nowhere to be seen. You'll be dealing with the artist's tour manager. It's the agent's job to pass on all necessary information to the artist's manager, by way of the contract. It's the manager's job to pass necessary information to the tour manager. Has everyone done his or her job? You won't know unless you establish a line of communication with the tour manager.

The tour manager's job is to be the jerk on the ground and raise hell if there's anything not to his or the band's liking. You really don't want to give him ammunition to do that by springing surprises on him at the last moment.

You also need to connect with your sound engineer, lighting director, and stage guy. You may have spoken to them months ago and assumed that they could set up on the day of the show. What happens when they all show up at the same time on the morning of the party?

Your lighting guy and your sound guy can't set up until they have a stage to set up on, so they will have nothing to do but cool their heels for two hours. This is exactly the kind of detail that should be addressed in the advance.

Imagine that your band shows up, and they want seven bottles of filtered water and a case of organic cigarettes. When you read their hospitality rider three months before the gig, those items weren't mentioned. You can stand on your rights and refuse to provide them what they want, but that's creating needless conflict with a group of people who will be performing for you in a few hours. Again, the advance is the time to catch this, before it becomes a major issue.

If your lighting designer needs more power than they originally anticipated, you want to find out during the advance, not on the day of the show. With a few days' notice, you can still make adjustments and call in some extra power. With only hours to work with, you're instantly in panic mode.

A thorough advance will relieve you of 99.9 percent of the nasty surprises that could otherwise trip you up at the last moment. There will always be an element of uncertainty. With live entertainment, that simply cannot be avoided, but it can be vastly reduced with an effective advance.

There's no value in performing an advance more than ten days before your event, because it won't be useful. There will still be too much time between the advance and the show for new problems to arise. By the same token, you need enough time between the advance and the show to address any new information that comes to light. Five to ten days before the event is an appropriate time for the advance.

If you were a soldier, you wouldn't go into battle with a dirty, rusty gun. Your life could depend upon making sure that all the components look and operate the way they're intended to. As a social chair, the stakes aren't quite as high, but the quality of your party depends upon executing an advance.

You may have had a game plan four months ago when you were planning this event, but now you need to knock the dust off. Now it's time to make sure all the moving parts are clean and ready to function. Don't go into battle without conducting an advance.

THIS IS YOUR SHOW

Unless you have delegated the production of your party to

a turnkey company or a production company, no one else will handle the advance for you.

On the day of the show, a lot of things need to happen in a very specific sequence and within a tight timescale. If the sequence and the schedule are not adhered to, problems will arise.

For example, you need to settle your bill with the artist. This should not be a particularly complicated process, because no tickets were sold. There are no percentages to be calculated or expenses to be deducted.

Even here, however, you can find yourself in unexpected situations. Maybe you agreed months ago that you would pay the artist with a check, but since then they've decided they want cash. What will you do at 11:00 p.m. on a Saturday night, when your entertainers want $5,000 in cash and you have an $800 limit on your ATM card?

Alternatively, perhaps they're happy with a check, but your treasurer is passed out upstairs with the door locked. What will you do?

When you advance your event, make sure that you include your own personal advance. Ensure that you know how and when you'll pay your artist, who is handling ground transportation and hospitality, and what happens to the stage when the show is over.

At 2:00 a.m., everybody will be exhausted, and probably hammered. The guys who have been working have been on duty for eleven hours. Do you have a plan for breaking down the stage? If not, you're potentially leaving $100,000 worth of gear outside to be rained on or stolen.

Make sure that you recap both your own responsibilities on the day of the show and the responsibilities of others. Hiring a turnkey company, of course, will make handling the advance their job instead of yours, although you will still need to make sure that it happens.

Compile a day sheet that details the responsibilities of each individual, and be so thorough that the people to whom you're delegating get annoyed with you. That way, they'll know that if they screw up, it's not from ignorance. It's on them. An ounce of prevention here is worth a pound of cure.

Do this with your sound engineer, lighting director, stage guy, stage manager, and security team. Now do the same with any of your fraternity brothers who have agreed to take on responsibilities. It's your job to make sure that they know what they're doing. By the day of the show, any details that were ironed out in the advance should be totally clear.

Some changes, however, are too important to be covered in the advance. If you plan to hold a party at your house, and then you realize that you need to move it to a different venue, you need to communicate this to your talent and your production team as soon as possible. Keeping it until the advance won't give them enough time to adapt.

In this situation, there could be issues that you're not even aware of, such as radius clauses. Your advance is a safety net, but it shouldn't prevent you from handling major issues when they emerge. Putting them off won't improve the situation—quite the reverse. They will come to a head at some point, so be a man and address them.

WHAT TO LOOK OUT FOR

There are many small details that could change during an advance and that you'll want to catch before they escalate into big problems.

For example, the band's load-in time could change. Maybe they were originally planning to drive in and set up their gear, but they had a nearby show canceled close to the date of the show. Now, instead of driving in with their own backline, they're flying in, and they want you to provide the backline (they should offer to let you deduct the cost of the backline from their total fee, or you can ask them to do so).

Previously, they needed two hours to set up their gear. Now, you'll have it all set up for them, so they only need to arrive forty-five minutes before the show kicks off.

If you used the phrase "per advance" when you made a formal offer, now is the time to revisit those aspects of the agreement and confirm them. You may encounter questions about what constitutes mutually agreeable hospitality, and the advance is the perfect time to hash those out. Perhaps one of the band members doesn't eat meat, so he needs a vegetarian option on the hospitality rider.

In case you struggle to reach an agreement, offer them a buyout and let them spend the money on whatever they choose. It's a lot easier, and simpler, than haggling over an acceptable quantity of red M&Ms and bottles of tequila. You can save money, because you will offer them half of what it would have cost you to meet their demands, and they'll have cash that they can spend however they choose.

When conducting an advance, make sure that you don't focus on advancing your artists to the exclusion of your production crew. You don't understand the terminology well enough to perform these advances yourself, but you need to make sure that they are connecting with the band's tour manager.

You can address this when you speak to the tour manager. Ask him whether he's spoken to the sound engineer and the lighting designer. If he tells you that he has, you've done your job. If he says he's been emailing for weeks and can't get a response, you need to step in.

To reiterate, the advance is an incredibly important part of your role, and it's the greatest service you can do to everyone involved: the performers, the production guys, your fraternity brothers, and every other attendee.

Even if you won't be able to enjoy the party as a participant, you will have the incredible satisfaction of knowing that you've created something beautiful. The advance is your ticket to a successful, smooth show, with an absolute minimum of unexpected last minute struggles.

You can reach the end of your show as a hero, knowing that you've exceeded the expectations of every person who was a part of it, or as a villain who messed up something crucial and turned it into a disaster. Don't walk into the lion's den without a solid advance.

THE DAY OF THE SHOW

—

This is it. Your victory march—or your funeral.

As long as you have advanced the show properly, the day itself should be comparatively smoother than if you had not.

You will need to be clearheaded and have a list in front of you of what is required. You will also need a full stomach. You have a long day ahead of you, and you need to be energetic.

Make sure that everyone else with responsibilities has a list of what's required of *them*, too. These are your day sheets. You should have organized everything before time and advanced it five to ten days ago. You're ready to go. Now it's time to execute.

Strange as it may sound, it can actually be a lot of fun to be on top of things and handle anything that goes awry. When you're not worried about a dozen things going wrong at once, taking care of the one thing that needs your attention can be an expression of how well you have everything under control.

Assuming you like doing this (and if you didn't, you probably would have subbed out by now), a minor mishap can be your opportunity to rise to the occasion and be a problem solver. You've chosen to take responsibility for producing this event, and this is your time to shine. Allow yourself to get excited about that.

Of course, this means that you don't get to make out with your girlfriend in the bushes. It means that you don't get to decide the show isn't vibing and go downtown to grab a burger. You don't even get to leave the venue to go top off the band's hospitality rider. You have to be a visible presence at your event.

Before the entertainment arrives, make sure that the checks are written and that you have some backup checks in case you spelled someone's name incorrectly and he needs a do-over. Keep adequate cash on hand in case there was a misunderstanding even in the advance.

Sometimes the same person who told you a check was fine four months ago told you the same thing four days ago, and was wrong both times. It happens. It's not your fault, but that's cold comfort when you've got performers asking for cash and you don't have it. It's a good idea, too, to have enough cash on hand to purchase any last-minute items you might need.

Get the hospitality rider in early, and keep the food and drinks cold. Not only is a disgusting hospitality setup a waste of good food, but it's also demoralizing for the band. They live on the road, and when all they want is some cold water and decent food and you're offering them lukewarm drinks and sandwiches that have been sitting in the sun all afternoon, it's disrespectful of their needs as human beings.

It hardly needs to be said that if you offer your band repulsive slop, it will affect their mood and probably their performance. Acknowledge your obligations and take care of the people who have come to play a great show for you.

In the event that it's your responsibility, organize ground transportation so that your artists aren't waiting to be picked up. Especially for bands that are at least somewhat famous, waiting around can be very annoying. They'll be accosted by every random sorority girl in the vicinity, wanting a selfie with them. You want them to be ready on time, so do them the courtesy of making sure that whoever is tasked with collecting them is also on time.

If you have more than one band on the bill, make sure that you have planned the schedule carefully. You've either hired a stage manager or you *are* the stage manager; if the latter, make sure that you have the right mind-set and energy to take the job on.

After the show, you still need to be alert enough to oversee breaking down the stage. There will be people wanting to be paid, and they will be looking at you. You need to have checks written or cash on hand.

Maybe you hired a tent to use as a green room, and the vendor asks you whether it's OK to come and get it on Monday morning. You want only to crawl into bed and sleep for a week, so you say yes, not realizing that your adviser and your neighbors won't be happy about your front yard looking like Jonestown on Sunday.

All the questions, and all the problems, will be coming to you. This is why you need to plan well, sleep well the night before the show, get a good meal inside you before you start, and stay sober. If you're exhausted, hungry, and then you get drunk, you won't have the mental energy to handle everything you need to be on top of.

Of course, many of these questions can and should be addressed in advance. You need to know how you will pay your vendors and who will handle the breakdown long before they're holding their hands out at 2:00 a.m. and you have a stage full of gear to deal with.

As long as you do that, the show should run smoothly, and you will give your fraternity brothers a memory they'll cherish for the rest of their lives. At the same time, you'll discover a sense of competence in yourself that can win you massive respect and leave you walking taller for months.

—

PART THREE

ASSISTANCE

"Hire people who are better than you are, then leave them to get on with it."

DAVID OGILVY

"Everyone has a plan until they get punched in the face."

MIKE TYSON

WHO CAN HELP YOU?

—

Maybe you've read through the book so far and decided that putting together your own event sounds like far more work than you're willing to undertake.

Maybe you skipped to this section straightaway because you already knew that.

Alternatively, maybe you want to take on most of the responsibility for your show, but you'd like some help with key elements of it.

This chapter will lay out the landscape of service providers in the industry, and it will let you know in detail what you can expect from each of them.

INDIVIDUAL SERVICE PROVIDERS

First of all, you have individual service providers. On the production side of your party, these are technicians and engineers, whether their specialties are lighting, audio, or stage rental.

These guys are gearheads. Their desire in life is to operate gear. They don't want to be businesspeople, they don't want to be salespeople, and sometimes when you communicate with them you may feel as though they don't particularly want to talk to people at all.

MIDDLE BUYERS

If you choose to produce your own event, you will need to work directly with the people listed above. You will also take on the role of talent buyer, communicating with agents and management to negotiate deals. Some of these services can be outsourced. Middle buyers, for example, will help you secure the services of the talent you want to book.

The advantage of using middle buyers is that they understand where you're coming from. The average middle buyer was probably a social chair himself a decade ago. He got recruited because he was the cool guy on campus. Now he's got two kids and all he does is hustle bands on behalf of current social chairs. He understands your situation, and at the same time he has connections with the bands you want to hire.

The middle buyer model is falling out of fashion because it has never been easier to approach agents directly. This doesn't mean that doing that is necessarily a good idea, only that it's an option.

Middle buyers operate using one of two approaches. The first is called a pass-through, where they broker deals on your behalf and retain a commission of 10–20 percent of the total fee. They don't take responsibility beyond brokering deals. They simply create a contract between you and the agent.

The alternative to a pass-through is known as a buy/sell. When you engage a middle buyer on a buy/sell basis, he will take your money and use it to make purchases.

You will usually find that a middle buyer using a buy/sell model will be more hands-on than one earning a commission from a pass-through, because she has an opportunity to maximize her profit.

Commission from a pass-through is set at a standard rate. You know that if you give a middle buyer a budget of $10,000, she will take a percentage of that fee. She probably won't show much interest in making sure that you have adequate production and staging, but she'll organize your talent.

With a buy/sell, a middle buyer can make a lot more money by finding better deals. If you give her $10,000, she'll try and find you a great band for $4,000 so she can spend $2,000 on production and pocket the rest, upping her profit margin to 40 percent.

As long as you're happy with the service, that's fine. You get what you want out of the deal, and so does the middle buyer. If you went in on your own, you couldn't get the deals she does, so it's still a win.

The only problem with this approach is that the temptation to cut corners can be enormous. Every cent your middle buyer saves from a buy/sell will go straight into her pocket, so she's more likely to book you a lower-quality stage or a less experienced sound engineer.

When engaging a middle buyer, you need to be sure that she is reputable; otherwise you risk lining her pockets. Nonetheless, a good middle buyer can bring you a lot of value. If she runs a pass-through for you, she probably won't get screwed in the same way you might, and if you trust her with a buy/sell, she can take care of a lot of the things that might cost you a lot of time and energy.

I would wager that anyone who refuses to tell you what she paid to hire a band, or a lighting designer, or a generator has something to hide. There's nothing wrong with making out like a bandit by calling in a favor and getting a great band at a heavily discounted price, but if your middle buyer can't look you in the eye and tell you the truth about the deals she's making, do you really want to work with her? Always seek out references before you engage a middle buyer.

PRODUCTION COMPANIES

On the production side of the equation, production companies can run point for you. At the most basic end of the market, they will provide a lighting designer, a sound engineer, and a stage technician. They will make sure that these people show up on time and in the right order.

Some people are interested in testing the waters in the talent market because they have a desire to better understand the industry. They want to know how it works, even if that means learning the hard way. Relatively few social chairs are interested in becoming production engineers.

For this reason, I encourage people to work with production companies and take the stress out of actually producing the show. Find a reputable production company and pay them good money to show up and deliver.

A lot of the people in production companies are more interested in nerding out on a great show than in making pots of cash. They have loads of gear sitting in a warehouse, and they want to put it to use. More often than not, you'll get more than you're paying for from these guys because their name is on the show and they want it to look and sound amazing.

If they were only interested in making money, they'd be in a different industry. They do what they do because they love it. A good production company can save you a lot of heartache.

As long as you can find a good company near you, hire locally. Big companies may brag about what they can do, but the downside is that they're driving in from an hour away. This means that you'll pay them for travel and lodging, either directly or via an increase in their pricing.

Ask yourself whether the service they're providing is worth the extra money. If the local company is good, but not great, maybe you can encourage them to become great so that they win more of your business. Obviously, if they suck, it's worth shelling out the extra for the guys who know what they're doing.

The biggest risk you run when hiring a production company is not that they'll try to rip you off financially, but that they'll get overexcited about the chance to use all their gear and try to sell you on equipment you don't really need.

Just because you can, that doesn't always mean you should. You don't want to be short of lighting or sound quality, but you also don't want to pay for technical specifications you really don't need. You want to achieve the biggest possible bang for your buck, and a good production company will give you that.

I've seen plenty of middle buyers screw people over. Their goal is to make money, and they probably won't come to the show anyway. I've never seen a production engineer pull those kinds of tricks. Perhaps that's because I've been particularly fortunate, but I think it's because production engineers love what they do, will be at the party, and will have their name on the work.

TURNKEY EVENT PRODUCERS

Turnkey is a full service that frees you to enjoy your show. If what you want out of your parties is to experience them with your friends, you need to engage a turnkey operation.

Turnkey combines the services of a production company and a middle buyer under one roof. These companies are less common for the simple reason that running an entire event for you is a lot of work.

The job of a turnkey company is to make sure that your vision reaches fruition. Unless you are totally clueless about how to proceed, it is not their job to steer the ship.

The biggest advantage of having a turnkey company on your team is that they take on the responsibility of making your party happen. Some will even take out a general liability insurance policy on the event. They know what they're doing, and they know they're responsible for its success.

This can be a huge burden off your shoulders. A turnkey organization cannot force a reluctant rapper to get on a plane, but they will have three backup plans ready to execute if something goes wrong. The fact that they take on so much risk and responsibility is a big asset.

You can expect to deliver 10–20 percent of your total budget to a turnkey company to secure their services. In other words, if you have a party budget of $10,000, they will take $1000 to $2000 to make it happen.

Ten percent is an incredible deal. In the world of corporate events, they can charge as much as 25–30 percent. In case you're not clear on your budget when you hire them, a turnkey company will simply take a percentage of every dollar spent in the production of your party.

The former option is preferable, because it ensures that you remain within an agreed budget.

Turnkey companies may not be the way to go if you're into the idea of producing an event and you want to do it all yourself. Perhaps you want to go into the music industry, and this is the greatest opportunity you'll ever have to produce an event using someone else's money.

On the other hand, if you tell a turnkey company that's your ambition, they should be happy to include you in the process. You may become their next employee or one of the agents they're reaching out to in a few years time.

If you want to become a talent buyer, or ultimately produce your own festival, working with a turnkey company can put you in close contact with people who already know how to do that. You can stand on the shoulders of giants and save yourself learning the hard way.

ESTABLISHING REPUTABILITY

As with every other player in the market, working with a turnkey company only serves you if you can locate a quality organization where the employees know what they're doing.

Don't be shy about doing your research and asking people

tough questions, whether you're talking to a middle buyer, a production company, a representative of a turnkey company, or any other vendor. Quiz them about the services they offer, and ask them how they make money. If their answers seem vague, press them for clarification.

You can't expect them to know the market value of a particular artist at any given time, but you can expect them to have access to that information. If they don't respond to your questions promptly, or you can't get solid information out of them, those are red flags.

Check out the websites of companies you're interested in, and their social media feeds. You want to work with people who are interested in your continued business, not merely in getting rich quick and getting out of Dodge.

One social chair I worked with asked me: "How are you planning on screwing me?" That's a great question, and you can tell a lot about a person or a company from the response they give.

I told this guy that I wanted to make a little bit of his money for the next twenty-five years, and we worked together profitably. If whomever you're thinking of working with can't give you a straight answer to that question, maybe they really *are* planning on screwing you.

Look out for sleazebags, don't be afraid to ask the hard questions, and you'll find the support you need to create an incredible event.

CONCLUSION

DONE

One of the first clients I ever worked with in Greek life was an exceptionally well-known fraternity. They didn't book the biggest acts or have the biggest budget, but their parties were epic. For the first party we worked on together, they were expecting thousands and thousands of people.

The previous year, things had gotten a little out of hand, and they sought us out to bring order to the chaos.

We tightened up the security and planned to set up two stages instead of one. Then we reached out to every regional band we could think of and told them that they had an opportunity to play in front of four thousand people, with the added bonus that we would shoot video footage of their performance.

After that, we went back to the fraternity and told them that we would record the event, in a way that highlighted all the best aspects of their party.

With two stages, we were able to coordinate the schedule so perfectly that there were no breaks in the sound. The moment one band strummed their final chord, the next struck their first note. There was a sea of people moving from one stage to another, having an amazing time.

In total, we booked fourteen bands across the two stages. By selling video packages to the entertainers themselves, we were able to cover the cost of making the recordings. The fraternity got a free promotional video, and the bands, several of which are now national acts, were still using the footage to demonstrate how they could command a crowd years later.

The following year, the same fraternity hired us again, this time with twice the budget. They simply hadn't realized what was possible. Once they did, their ambitions skyrocketed.

We produced a day festival for them, with multiple stages and a roster of up-and-coming bands. That was five years ago. Nowadays, the party is *huge*, and it's still getting bigger. It's lost the sleazy air it had when we stepped in, and it has the potential to grow even more.

When people saw what was possible, the chapter decided to direct more of their budget toward the event. Social chairs are always battling to secure funding. The big takeaway from this show is that, when you demonstrate to people what's possible with their money, they'll be willing to give you more.

Additionally, fraternity parties are coming under constant scrutiny. In the age of smartphones, we all are. Sometimes it's warranted, and sometimes parties get shut down or stopped simply because they get a bit out of control.

By cleaning up an event that was heading in the wrong direction, we turned it around and made it stronger than ever. Now it has a great reputation and has become a highly anticipated event throughout the community.

On another occasion, we were working with a very large chapter fraternity to produce a massive event. They could book almost any artist they set their minds to, but the one they wanted wasn't available.

What do you do when the going gets tough? Think outside the box. The entertainer they wanted to book was doing a sponsored private event for Coca-Cola. The event was taking place in the same town as the party we were putting together, with no radius clause, a week after the scheduled date of the show.

We approached the band and told them that, yes, we knew that they were worth $25,000, but we also knew that they were going to be in town anyway. We had $12,000. If we moved the event back a week, would they perform for us on the Saturday after their sponsored Friday night gig for Coca-Cola?

Twenty-four hours later, they came back to us and told us that we had to sign an agreement stating that we would not talk about or otherwise promote the show, and that we would not disclose what we were paying them. Our client said: "Great, where do I sign?" They got an awesome show from a $25,000 act for $12,000. Today, the same act is booking for $50,000.

Sometimes, if you want to make an impact in a certain field, you need to manufacture your own reality. In this case, we found a way to ride the coattails of another event to bring in an act that would otherwise have been way beyond our client's price range.

If you've read this book from cover to cover, you know exactly how to go about creating a party just like those I described above, one that will bring honor to your chapter and envy to every other fraternity. If you've chosen to thumb through this book, you have an idea of what's possible and, hopefully, big ideas that you're excited to execute.

You can use it as a reference to guide you on the journey, and then pass it on to someone else who can benefit from it.

Ultimately, the aim of this book is to educate people so that they have cooler, safer events and get better value for their money. In case you come across something that you think is missing, you can email me at questions@treymyers.com and let me know. Perhaps your suggestion will make it into a future edition.

To learn more about Turnipblood Entertainment, take a look at the company website, www.turnipbloodent.com. I'm always happy to talk with you about anything you've read in this book, answer any questions you may have, and point you in the direction of specialists who handle any aspects of your business that we don't get involved with.

A FINAL WORD

Ten years ago, half the bands we worked with wouldn't even have considered playing fraternity houses. The landscape has changed so dramatically that any kind of live entertainment that will further their careers and give them a payday has started to look more appealing.

The situation for artists is not getting any better. Opportunities to earn money are becoming fewer and farther between. The recording industry has tanked, and even the lucrative festival scene is becoming diluted and losing attendees.

For that reason, I think private events will only continue to grow as a source of amazing entertainment for partygoers and a solid revenue stream for artists. There are many technological advances, but the principles are constant. Every private event requires someone to book the talent and a team to organize and run the production.

The desire to create and the desire to be entertained will not die, but the medium in which they are expressed will continue to evolve.

Don't be afraid to think outside the box and make extraordinary things happen. Twenty years ago, it would have been impossible to predict the growth and development of fraternity parties. Who knows what will be possible in another decade or two?

These are exciting times.

ABOUT THE AUTHOR

TREY MYERS is the president and founder of Turnipblood Entertainment, a full-service private events company specializing in Greek life. Over the course of 7 years in the entertainment industry, Trey has worked in various capacities at leading agencies, including the Agency For The Performing Arts (APA), The Agency Group (now owned by United Talent Agency), and Nimbleslick Entertainment.

Trey's other experiences include artist management, tour management, event production, and promotions. Prior to his return to the music business in 2010, Trey spent two years working on Capitol Hill and one year as an organic farmer. He lives with his family in east Nashville, Tennessee.

65853898R00130

Made in the USA
Charleston, SC
10 January 2017